WHAT THE REVIEWERS SAY

Had more traditional finance professionals been reading the psychology literature and/or taken the early writings in behavioral finance more seriously, the recent extreme volatility and overpricing in certain market sectors might have been ameliorated, or at least, better understood.

This book is a must read for everyone interested in better understanding how people, and thus markets, function.

—*Linda Martin, Arizona State University*

I found John Nofsinger's book loaded with common sense advice! Personally, it helped me to let go of bad investments and move on to logical versus emotional choices.

—*Holly Roge, Information Systems Consultant*

Investment Madness provides great insight into how the way we think impacts how we invest. A must read for all investors!

—*Dr. Brian Prucyk, Marquette University*

Investment Madness is an extremely insightful book. An absolute read for the beginning or experienced investor. I'm often asked by my clients for recommendations on books about investing. This will be #1 on my list!

—*E. Scott Tinder, Financial Advisor, American Express*

A new perspective on investing that will benefit professionals and the individual investor!

—*Dr. Jerome A. Mahalick, CEO, Asset Management for Professionals*

Every investor thinks he or she can beat the market. In fact, as this book shows, most don't. Sometimes funny, sometimes frightening, John Nofsinger's analysis of the psychological traps into which investors fall should be required reading for anyone thinking of venturing onto Wall Street.

—*Morgan Witzel, Editor-in-Chief, Corporate Finance Review*

FINANCIAL TIMES
Prentice Hall

In an increasingly competitive world, it is quality
of thinking that gives an edge. An idea that opens new
doors, a technique that solves a problem, or an insight
that simply helps make sense of it all.

We must work with leading authors in the fields of
management and finance to bring cutting-edge thinking
and best learning practice to a global market.

Under a range of leading imprints, including
Financial Times Prentice Hall, we create world-class
print publications and electronic products giving readers
knowledge and understanding which can then be
applied, whether studying or at work.

To find out more about our business and professional
products, you can visit us at www.phptr.com

Pearson
Education

Investment Madness

How Psychology Affects Your Investing...and What to Do About It

ISBN 0-13-042200-2

90000

9 780130 422002

FINANCIAL TIMES PRENTICE HALL BOOKS

James W. Cortada
   *21st Century Business: Managing and Working in
   the New Digital Economy*

Aswath Damodaran
   *The Dark Side of Valuation: Valuing OldTech, New Tech,
   and New Economy Companies*

Deirdre Breakenridge
   Cyberbranding: Brand Building in the Digital Economy

Dale Neef
   e-Procurement: From Strategy to Implementation

John R. Nofsinger
   *Investment Madness: How Psychology Affects Your Investing...
   and What to Do About It*

Investment Madness

How Psychology Affects Your Investing...and What to Do About It

John R. Nofsinger
Washington State University

FINANCIAL TIMES
Prentice Hall

An Imprint of PEARSON EDUCATION
London • New York • San Francisco • Toronto
Sydney • Tokyo • Singapore • Hong Kong • Cape Town
Madrid • Paris • Milan • Munich • Amsterdam

Library of Congress Cataloging-in-Publication Data

Nofsinger, John R.
    Investment madness : how psychology affects your investing—and what to do about it / John R. Nofsinger.
       p. cm.—(Financial Times Prentice Hall books)
       Includes bibliographical references and index.
       ISBN 0-13-042200-2 (case)
       1. Investments—Psychological aspects. 2. Investments—Decision making.
I. Title. II Series.

HG4515.15 .N64 2001
332.6'01'9—dc21

2001024614

Editorial/production supervision: BooksCraft, Inc., Indianapolis, IN
Acquisitions editor: Tim Moore
Editorial assistant: Allyson Kloss
Marketing manager: Tc Leszczynski
Manufacturing manager: Maura Zaldivar
Cover design director: Jerry Votta
Cover designer: Anthony Gemmellaro
Cover illustrator: Tom Post
Project coordinator: Anne Renee Garcia

©2001 by Prentice Hall
Prentice Hall, Inc.
Upper Saddle River, NJ 07458

Prentice Hall books are widely used by corporations and government agencies for training, marketing, and resale.

The publisher offers discounts on this book when ordered in bulk quantities. For more information, contract: Corporate Sales Department, Phone: 800-382-3419; Fax: 201-236-7141; E-mail: corpsales@prenhall.com; or write: Prentice Hall PTR, Corp. Sales Dept. One Lake Street, Upper Saddle River, NJ 07458

Product and company names mentioned herein are the trademarks of their respective owners.

Printed in the United States of America

10 9 8 7 6 5 4 3 2 1

ISBN 0-13-042200-2

Pearson Education Ltd.
Pearson Education Australia PTY, Ltd.
Pearson Education Singapore, Pte. Ltd.
Pearson Education North Asia Ltd.
Pearson Education Canada, Ltd.
Pearson Educación de Mexico, S.A. de C.V.
Pearson Education—Japan
Pearson Education Malaysia, Pte. Ltd.
Pearson Education, Upper Saddle River, New Jersey

TABLE OF CONTENTS

INTRODUCTION   xi

Chapter 1	**Your Behavior Matters!**	2

Why Haven't I Heard of This Before?   4
A Simple Illustration   4
Prediction   5
Behavioral Finance   8
The Investment Environment   8
Endnotes   10

1 NOT THINKING CLEARLY   11

Chapter 2	**Overconfidence**	12

Becoming Overconfident   14
Illusion of Knowledge   14
Illusion of Control   18
Recipe for Disaster?   19
Endnotes   20

Chapter 3	**Overconfidence and Investing**	22

Overconfidence: A Case Study1   23
Overconfidence and Trade Frequency   25
Gender Differences   25
Trading *Too* Much   26
Overconfidence and Risk   28
Overconfidence and Experience   29
Mutual Funds   30
Overconfidence and the Internet   30
Summing Up   31
Endnotes   32

Chapter 4	**Status Quo—Or What I Own Is Better!**	34

Endowment Effect   35
Endowment and Investing   36
Status Quo Bias   37
Attachment Bias   40
Overcoming These Biases   41
Endnotes   43

2 EMOTIONS RULE   45

Chapter 5   **Seeking Pride and Avoiding Regret**   46

Disposition Effect   47
Do We Really Sell Winners?   49
Selling Winners Too Soon and Holding Losers
   Too Long   51
The Disposition Effect and the Media   51
Avoiding the Avoiding of Regret   52
In Summary   54
Endnotes   55

Chapter 6   **Double or Nothing**   56

House-Money Effect   57
Snake-Bit (Risk-Aversion) Effect   58
Break-Even Effect   59
Would You Buy This IPO?   60
The Tech Bubble   62
Endnotes   64

Chapter 7   **Social Aspects of Investing**   66

Sharing Investment Knowledge   67
Moving with the Herd   68
Speed Is of the Essence (Not)   69
Investment Clubs   71
Beardstown Ladies   71
Investment Club Performance   72
Investment Clubs and Social Dynamics   73
Summing Up   74
Endnotes   75

3 FUNCTIONING OF THE BRAIN   77

Chapter 8   **Mental Accounting**   78

Mental Budgeting   80
Matching Costs to Benefits   80
Aversion to Debt   82
Sunk-Cost Effect   82
Economic Impact   84
Mental Accounting and Investing   84
Endnotes   86

Chapter 9	**Mental Accounting and Diversification**	**88**
	Mental Accounting and Portfolios	**89**
	Risk Perceptions	**91**
	Risk Perception in the Real World	**96**
	Building Behavioral Portfolios	**96**
	Summing Up	**98**
	Endnotes	**99**

Chapter 10	**That's Not the Way I Remember It**	**100**
	Memory and Investment Decisions	**102**
	Cognitive Dissonance	**103**
	Cognitive Dissonance and Investing	**104**
	Cognitive Dissonance and the Steadman Funds	**105**
	Memory and Socialization	**106**
	Reference Points	**107**
	Summing Up	**109**
	Endnotes	**110**

Chapter 11	**What I Know Is Better**	**112**
	Representativeness	**113**
	Representativeness and Investing	**114**
	Familiarity	**116**
	Familiarity Breeds Investment	**117**
	Familiarity Breeds Investment Problems	**119**
	Endnotes	**121**

4 INVESTING AND THE INTERNET — **123**

Chapter 12	**The Internet (Psycho) Investor**	**124**
	The Rise of the Internet Investor	**125**
	Amplifying Psychological Biases	**126**
	Information and Control	**126**
	Online Trading and Overconfidence	**128**
	Advertising—Increasing the Biases	**129**
	Online Trading and Performance	**130**
	Day Traders—The Extreme Case	**130**
	Summing Up	**132**
	Endnotes	**133**

Chapter 13	**Exuberance on (and about) the Net**	**134**
	A Rose.com by Any Other Name	135
	A Bubble Burst	137
	The More Things Change...	138
	The Boiler Room Goes Online	140
	Endnotes	143

5 WHAT CAN I DO ABOUT IT?   145

Chapter 14	**Self-Control, or the Lack of It!**	**146**
	Short-Term versus Long-Term Focus	148
	Controlling Ourselves	148
	Rules of Thumb	148
	Environment Control	149
	Self-Control and Saving	150
	IRAs	151
	401(k) Plans	151
	Self-Control and Investing	152
	Self-Control and Dividends	153
	Summing Up	155
	Endnotes	156

Chapter 15	**Battling Your Biases**	**158**
	Strategy 1: Understand Your Psychological Biases	159
	Not Thinking Clearly	159
	Letting Emotions Rule	161
	Functioning of the Brain	162
	Strategy 2: Know Why You Are Investing	163
	Strategy 3: Have Quantitative Investment Criteria	165
	Strategy 4: Diversify	166
	Strategy 5: Control Your Investing Environment	166
	Additional Rules of Thumb	168
	In Conclusion	169

INDEX   171

INTRODUCTION

We are all prone to having psychological preconceptions or biases that make us behave in certain ways. These biases influence how we assimilate the information we come in contact with on a daily basis. They also have an impact on how we utilize that information to make decisions.

Some of the decisions that are influenced by our psychological biases can have a large impact on our personal wealth—or the lack of it. I have written this book to try to show you how your own psychological biases can creep into your investment decisions and sabotage your attempts at building wealth.

WHAT TO EXPECT FROM THIS BOOK

There are five parts in this book. The first three parts illustrate different psychological biases that affect our daily lives. The chapters in these parts are structured so they are similar to each other. First, I identify the psychological trait and explain using common, daily activities. Then I examine the degree to which investors are affected by the bias. Part 4 demonstrates how the Internet exacerbates these psychological problems. Finally, the chapters in Part 5 describe what investors can do to help themselves.

The chapters in Part 1, "Not Thinking Clearly," demonstrate how investment decision making is not always rational. As you will see, people set their range of possible outcomes too narrowly. This is part of a broader problem called *overconfidence*. Overconfident investors trade too much, take too much risk, and earn lower returns. This topic is discussed in Chapters 2 and 3. If overconfidence causes investors to act too frequently, other biases described in Chapter 4 cause investors to fail to act when they should.

Part 2, "Emotions Rule," shows how the emotions associated with investing affect our decisions. Chapter 5 illustrates how an investor's view of himself causes him to avoid feelings of regret and to seek pride. Consequently, investors sell winner stocks too soon and hold onto loser stocks too long. Chapter 6 demonstrates that your past failures and successes have a dramatic impact on your current decision making process. Lastly, our emotional state is often affected by the social aspects of investing; we discuss this in Chapter 7.

The third part, "Functioning of the Brain," shows how the human brain's processes for interpreting and remembering information affect investors. For example, every day you are bombarded by information. The brain uses a process called *mental accounting* to store and keep track of important decisions and outcomes. Chapter 8 shows that as a consequence of this process, people make poor financial decisions. Discussed in Chapter 9 is one particularly important implication of how investors view portfolio diversification. The brain also uses shortcuts to quickly process information. These shortcuts create a tainted view of the information. This leads to impacts on investor memory (Chapter 10) and the problems of *representativeness* and *familiarity* (Chapter 11).

Part 4, "Investing and the Internet," discusses the interaction among the Internet, psychology, and investing. The Internet allows investors quick access to information, trading, and other investors' opinions. However, these attributes actually magnify the psychological biases. These issues are addressed in Chapters 12 and 13.

Finally, Part 5, "What Can I Do About It?" discusses what the investor can do to avoid these psychological biases. The difficulty of maintaining *self-control* in the face of these psychological biases is illustrated in Chapter 14. The last chapter shows that planning, incentives, and rules of thumb are helpful in avoiding the common problems.

DO YOU HAVE A STORY?

This book is for investors everywhere. Do you have a story to tell? You can contact me at *www.psychoinvestor.com*.

> Do not succumb to the status quo
> Read this book so that you will know
> How to let your investments grow

ACKNOWLEDGMENTS

I am grateful to many people who helped me with this book. The writing process has been a team effort. I feel fortune to have such a great team. Tim Moore kept the publishing process moving smoothly, while Russ Hall managed the writing process. The insights provided by Morgen Witzel and Holly Roge were particularly useful.

Family, friends, and students were exposed to this material in various ways. I thank them for providing feedback.

I would also like to thank two people who helped to get the project started—Dave Ungerman and Maureen Riopelle.

Investment Madness

How Psychology Affects Your Investing...and What to Do About It

1 Your Behavior Matters!

Milestones

- Why Haven't I Heard of This Before?
- Behavioral Finance
- The Investment Environment

If you are tempted to answer   **Should I read this book now, or later?**
"Later," then you should
consider reading Chapter 14, "Self-Control, or the Lack of It,"
first. As humans, we are prone to specific psychological
biases—procrastination is a good example—that can cause us
to behave in ways that reduce our wealth. These biases also
cause us to delay taking actions that would maximize our
wealth. Consider the following choices many people have.
How many times will they choose the delayed actions?

- Should I start contributing to my 401(k) plan now, or later?
- Should I invest the extra money that's in my savings account now, or later?
- Should I change the bonds and CDs I inherited to stocks now, or later?

In each of these cases, it is better to get the money invested
sooner. The longer your money is invested, the larger your
portfolio will grow.

However, a bias toward procrastination causes employees to delay making 401(k) pension plan decisions—often
losing time and employer contributions. People's bias
toward the status quo allows substantial money to build up
in savings accounts before it is transferred to investment
accounts; therefore they lose the higher returns an investment account offers. We also have a bias toward keeping the
securities we inherit instead of investing them in vehicles
that are more appropriate to our needs (the *endowment
effect*).

Not only does our psychology cause us to delay some
actions, it also can cause us to act too soon, too often, and
too badly in some cases. In investing, sometimes we act too
soon and sometimes we delay too long. Is this a paradox?
Probably, but that is because we are human.

WHY HAVEN'T I HEARD OF THIS BEFORE?

Much of the education for investors originates with the work of financial economists in the nation's universities. However, these financial economists have traditionally dismissed the idea that people's own psychology can work against them when it comes to making good investment decisions. For the past three decades, the field of finance has evolved on two basic assumptions:

- People make rational decisions.
- People are unbiased in their predictions about the future.

However, psychologists have known for a long time that these are bad assumptions. People often act in a seemingly irrational manner and make predicable errors in their forecasts.

Financial economists are now realizing that investors can be irrational. Indeed, predictable errors by investors can affect the function of the markets. But, most important to you, your reasoning errors affect your investing, and ultimately your wealth!

It is my opinion that you could completely understand all the information in a modern investment text but could still fail as an investor if you let your psychological biases control your decisions. This book

- Explains many psychological biases that affect decision making
- Shows how these biases can affect your investment decisions
- Helps you see how these decisions can reduce your wealth
- Teaches you how to recognize and avoid these biases in your own life

The rest of this chapter is dedicated to illustrating that these psychological problems are real. The arguments will be far more convincing if you participate in the demonstrations in the following two sections.

A Simple Illustration

One example of the reasoning mistakes caused by the brain is the visual illusion. Consider the optical illusion in Figure 1.1. Of the two horizontal lines, which looks longer?

In fact, both lines are the same length. Look again. Although you

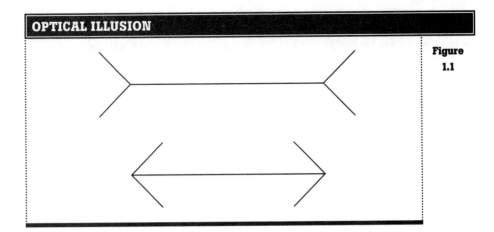

OPTICAL ILLUSION

Figure 1.1

know that the horizontal lines are equal in length, the top line still *looks* longer. Just knowing about the illusion does not eliminate it. However, if you had to make some decision based on these lines, knowing that it is an illusion would help you avoid a mistake.

Prediction

The brain does not work like a computer. Instead, it frequently processes information through shortcuts and emotional filters to shorten the analysis time. The decision arrived at through this process is often not the same decision you would make without these filters. I refer to these filters and shortcuts as psychological biases. Knowing about these psychological biases is the first step toward avoiding them. One common problem is overestimating the precision and importance of information. This demonstration illustrates this problem.

Let's face it, investing is difficult. You must make decisions based on information that may be inadequate or inaccurate. Additionally, you must be able to effectively understand and analyze the information. Unfortunately, people make predictable errors in their forecasts.

Consider the 10 questions in Figure 1.2.[1] Although you probably do not know the answers to these questions, enter a range in which you think the answer lies. Specifically, give your best low guess and your best high guess so that you are 90% sure the answer lies between the two. Don't make the range so wide that the answer is guaranteed to lie within, but also don't make the range too narrow. If you consistently make a range so that you are 90% sure the answer lies within, then you should expect to get 9 of the 10 questions correct.

DIFFICULTY OF PROCESSING AND EVALUATING INFORMATION— A DEMONSTRATION

Figure 1.2

Enter the range (minimum and maximum) within which you are 90% certain the answer lies.

	Min	Max
1. What is the average weight of the adult blue whale, in pounds?	____	____
2. In what year was the Mona Lisa painted by Leonardo da Vinci?	____	____
3. How many independent countries were there at the end of 2000?	____	____
4. What is the air distance, in miles, between Paris, France, and Sydney, Australia?	____	____
5. How many bones are in the human body?	____	____
6. How many total combatants were killed in World War I?	____	____
7. How many books were in the Library of Congress at the end of 2000?	____	____
8. How long, in miles, is the Amazon River?	____	____
9. How fast does the earth spin (miles per hour) at the equator?	____	____
10. How many transistors are in the Pentium III computer processor?	____	____
	____	____

If you have no idea of the answer to a question, then your range should be large in order to be 90% confident. On the other hand, if you think you can give a good educated guess, then you can choose a smaller range and still be 90% confident. Go ahead now—give it your best shot.

Most people miss five or more questions. However, if you are 90% sure of your range, then you should have missed only one. The fact is that we are too certain about our answers, even when we have no information or knowledge about the topic. Even being educated in probability and statistics is no help. Most finance professors miss at least five of the questions too!

This demonstration illustrates that people have difficulty effectively processing and evaluating information.

Now let's check the answers. They are (1) 250,000 pounds; (2) 1513; (3) 191 countries; (4) 10,543 miles; (5) 206 bones; (6) 8.3 million; (7) 18 million; (8) 4,000 miles; (9) 1,044 miles per hour; and (10) 9.5 million. Count your response correct if the answer lies between your low and high guesses. How many did you get right?

Now that I have shown you the difficulty, let's try another one. Since this book relates psychology to investing, consider the following question:

> In 1896 the Dow Jones Industrial Average (DJIA) was 40. At the end of 1998, the DJIA was 9,181. The DJIA is a price-weighted average. Dividends are omitted from the index. What would the DJIA average be at the end of 1998 if the dividends were reinvested each year?

Notice that Figure 1.2 has room for your DJIA minimum and maximum guesses. Again, pick a range in which you are 90% sure the answer lies. You should get this one correct. Ready for the answer?

If dividends were reinvested in the DJIA, the average would have been 652,230 at the end of 1998.[2] Does this surprise you? It surprises most people. Even after learning that most people set too narrow a range in their predictions, and even after experiencing the problem firsthand, most people continue to make the same mistake!

Long Term Capital Management Hedge Fund Even Nobel prize winners in economics are prone to overestimating the precision of their knowledge. Consider the plight of the hedge fund Long Term Capital Management (LTCM). The partners of the fund included John Meriwether, the famed bond trader from Salomon Brothers; David Mullins, a former vice chairman of the Federal Reserve Board; and Nobel prize winners Myron Scholes and Robert Merton. The firm employed 24 people with Ph.D.s.

The hedge fund began in 1994 and enjoyed stellar returns. In the beginning of 1998, LTCM had $4 billion in equity. It had also borrowed $100 billion to leverage its positions for higher returns. Its original strategy was to find arbitrage opportunities in the bond market. These are low-risk strategies that usually garner low returns. However, since they were so highly leveraged, the low returns were magnified into high returns. After several years of great success, LTCM found fewer arbitrage opportunities. At that point, the hedge fund began entering into riskier positions. The risk was compounded by the high leverage from borrowing.

In August of 1998, Russia devalued its currency and defaulted on some of its debt. This action started a chain of events over the next four weeks that led to devaluation in many emerging countries. Bond and stock markets around the world declined. The prices of U.S. Treasury securities skyrocketed as investors fled to the safest investments.

These events caused the equity in the LTCM portfolio to fall from $4 billion to $0.6 billion in one month. The Federal Reserve Bank feared that a margin call on LTCM would force it to liquidate its $100 billion worth of positions. The selling of these positions during this precarious time might precipitate a crisis that could endanger the financial system. By late September, a consortium of leading investment and commercial banks injected $3.5 billion into the fund in exchange for 90% of the equity.

How could a hedge fund with such brainpower lose 90% of its equity in one month? Apparently, in designing their models, the fund's masterminds did not think that so many things could go wrong at the same time. Doesn't this sound like their range of possible outcomes was too narrow?

BEHAVIORAL FINANCE

All people (even smart ones) are affected by psychological biases. However, traditional finance has considered this irrelevant. Traditional finance assumes that people are rational and tells us how people should behave in order to maximize their wealth. These ideas have brought us arbitrage theory, portfolio theory, asset pricing theory, and option pricing theory.

Alternatively, behavioral finance studies how people actually behave in a financial setting. Specifically, it is the study of how psychology affects financial decisions, corporations, and the financial markets. This book focuses on a subset of these issues—how psychological biases affect investors.

THE INVESTMENT ENVIRONMENT

This information is very timely because the current investment environment magnifies our psychological biases. Several powerful forces have affected investors recently. First, a strong and extended economy has created the disposable income for millions of new investors to enter the investment world. Most of these new investors have little or no formal education in finance. Second, this economy has spurred one of the longest and strongest bull markets in history. These new investors could have mistakenly attributed their high investment returns to their own capabilities instead of being a consequence of investing during a bull market. Finally, the rise of the Internet has led to increased investor participation in the investment process, allowing investors to trade, research, and chat online. These three factors have helped our psychological biases to flourish.

These ideas are well demonstrated by the cartoon in Figure 1.3 in which a roller coaster represents the modern investment environment. This roller coaster, like our stock market, has dramatic highs and lows. We go from a high to a low and back again these days at what seems like frightening speeds. Remember how you felt after your first roller coaster ride? The roller coaster causes strong emotions. Some people feel terrified while others are exuberant. Some people never ride another roller coaster, while others become addicted and wish to ride over and over again. Our new investment environment can also elicit emotions and enhance our natural psychological biases. These attributes usually lead to bad decisions. The rest of this book demonstrates these problems.

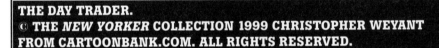

Figure 1.3

ENDNOTES

1. This exercise is similar to that of Hersh Shefrin, 2000, *Beyond Greed and Fear*, Boston, Massachusetts: Harvard Business School Press.

2. Roger Clarke and Meir Statman, 2000, "The DJIA Crossed 652,230," *Journal of Portfolio Management*, Winter: 89–93.

1

Not Thinking Clearly

(2) Overconfidence

Milestones

- Becoming Overconfident
- Recipe for Disaster?

People are overconfident. Psychologists have determined that overconfidence causes people to overestimate their knowledge, underestimate risks, and exaggerate their ability to control events. Does overconfidence occur in investment decision making? Security selection is a difficult task. It is precisely this type of task at which people exhibit the greatest overconfidence.

Are you overconfident?

How many questions did you answer right in the previous chapter? If you selected a correct range nine or more times, then you may not be overconfident. However, I have asked these questions to many groups, and *no one* has answered nine or more correctly. Most people are overconfident about their abilities. Consider the following question.

> How good a driver are you? Compared to the drivers you encounter on the road, are you above average, average, or below average?

How would you answer this question? If overconfidence were not involved, approximately one-third of those reading this book would answer above average, one-third would answer average, and one-third would answer below average. However, people are overconfident in their abilities. Most people feel that they are above average. When groups of students, professors, professionals, and investment club members were asked this question, nearly everyone answered that they are above average. Clearly, many of them are mistaken and are overconfident about their skill in driving.

Being overconfident in driving may not be a problem that affects your life. However, people are overconfident about their skill in many things. Sometimes overconfidence can affect your financial future.

Consider this financially oriented example. Starting a business is a very risky venture; in fact, most new businesses fail. When 2,994 new business owners were asked about their chance of success, they thought they had a 70% chance of success. But only 39% of these new owners thought that a business like theirs would be as likely to succeed.[1] Why do new business owners think they have nearly twice the chance of success as others in the same business? They are overconfident.

BECOMING OVERCONFIDENT

We begin the process when we enter a new activity, say, investing. We do not know our ability at investing, so we observe the consequences

Unlike many psychological biases, overconfidence is learned.

of our investment decisions. If we are successful, it is human nature to attribute that success to our ability. But not all success comes from high ability. Indeed, some successes come from dumb luck.

Consider the Dartboard column frequently run by the *Wall Street Journal*. Periodically, the *Wall Street Journal* invites four or five investment analysts to pick a stock for purchase. Simultaneously, they pick four or five other stocks by throwing darts at the financial pages. They follow the analysts' stocks and the dartboard stocks and report the returns produced by both sets. More likely than not, the dartboard portfolio beats the pros. Does the dart thrower have superior stock-picking ability? No, it's just that dumb luck success is common.

People investing during the late 1990s probably experienced great returns—it is easy to earn high returns during a strong, extended bull market. Many new investors began investing during this period. The problem arises when the newer investors attribute their success to their ability. Thus the old Wall Street adage warning "Don't confuse brains with a bull market!"

Psychologists have found that people become overconfident when they experience early success in a new activity. Also, having more information available and a higher degree of control leads to higher overconfidence. These factors are referred to as the *illusion of knowledge* and the *illusion of control*.

Illusion of Knowledge

People have the tendency to believe that the accuracy of their forecasts increases with more information. This is the illusion of knowledge—that more information increases your knowledge about something and improves your decisions. However, this is not always the case—increased levels of information do not necessarily lead to greater knowledge. There are three reasons for this. First, some information does not help us make predictions and can even mislead us. Second, many people may not have the training, experience, or skills to interpret the information. And, finally, people tend to interpret new information as confirmation of their prior beliefs.

To illustrate the first point, I roll a fair six-sided die. What number do you think will come up and how sure are you that you are right? Clearly, you can pick any number between 1 and 6 and have a one-sixth chance of being right. What if I told you that the last three rolls of the die have each produced the number 4? If I roll the die again, what number do you think will come up, and what chance do you have of being right?

If the die is truly fair, then you could still pick any number between 1 and 6 and have a one-sixth chance of being correct, regardless of what previous rolls have produced. The added information will not increase your ability to forecast the roll of the die. However, many people will believe that the number 4 has a greater (than one-sixth) chance to be rolled again. Others will believe that the number 4 has a lower chance to be rolled again. Both groups of people will think that their chance of being right is higher than reality. That is, the new information makes people more confident in their predictions, even though their chances for being correct do not change.

What return do you think the firm TechCron will earn next year? Don't know? Last year TechCron earned 38% and it earned 45% the year before that. Now what return would you guess?

Of course, TechCron is just a made-up firm, so you have no other information. But how is this example any different from rolling the die? Frankly, it is not different. Yet, investors commonly use past returns as one of the primary factors to predict the future. Have you switched your money into one of last year's best mutual funds?

Investors have access to vast quantities of information. This information includes historical data like past prices, returns, and corporate operational performance, as well as current information like real-time news, prices, and volume. Individual investors have access to information on the Internet that is nearly as good as the information available to professional investors. *Because most individual investors lack the training and experience of professional investors they are less equipped to know how to interpret information.* They may *think* they have access to all this incredible inside information and that may well be true, but, without the proper training, they cannot begin to guess how that information might shape the future— any more than they can guess future rolls of the die from what was rolled in the past.

The cartoon in Figure 2.1 illustrates this point. What is that guy saying? What does it mean? What should I do now that I have the information?

The last reason information does not lead to knowledge: People have a tendency to interpret new information as a confirmation of their prior beliefs. *Instead of being objective, people look for the information that confirms their earlier decisions.* Consider what happens

Figure 2.1

STEVENSON

"O.K. The forward rate for marks rose in March and April, combined with a sharp increase in German reserves and heavy borrowing in the Eurodollar market, while United States liquid reserves had dropped to fourteen billion dollars, causing speculation that the mark might rise and encouraging conversion on a large scale. *Now* do you understand?"

after a company reports lower earnings than expected—the price usually falls quickly, followed by high volume. High volume means that many people decided to sell and others decided to buy.

Consider an earnings warning by Microsoft Corporation. Microsoft warned that earnings would be closer to 42¢ a share instead of the expected 49¢. This warning was issued while the stock market was closed. What would you have done? As Figure 2.2 indicates, the opening trade for Microsoft was down $4.50 to $51 a share. When earnings information is released, prices quickly reflect the new consensus on the company. Note on Figure 2.2 that, after the initial price drop, the price hardly changed at all during the next hour of trading. If you think that Microsoft is not a very good investment, then the earnings warning probably induced you to sell. However, by the time you sold, you had already lost $4.50 a share. The only reason you would have sold after finding out about the price drop is if you thought that Microsoft would not be a good investment in the future. Or you might have felt that Microsoft *is* a good investment and used this warning as an opportunity to buy in at a low price. A lot of people were induced to trade on this news—nearly 1.9 million shares were traded in the first 5 minutes. Over half a million shares

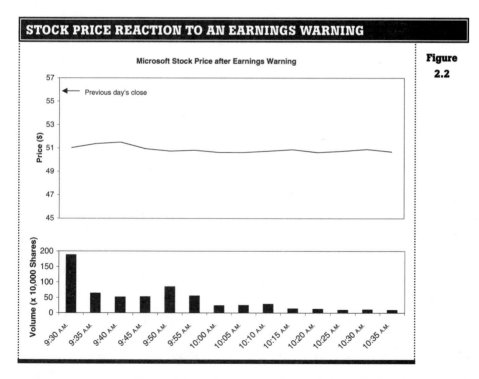

STOCK PRICE REACTION TO AN EARNINGS WARNING

Microsoft Stock Price after Earnings Warning

Figure 2.2

were traded every 5 minutes during the next 25 minutes of trading. Clearly, many investors wanted to sell and many others wanted to buy. One news report caused two different behaviors.

Illusion of Control

People become even more overconfident when they *feel* like they have control of the outcome—even when this is clearly not the case.

For example—and this has been documented—if you ask people to bet on whether a coin toss will end in heads or tails, most will bet larger amounts if you ask for the bet before the coin has been tossed. If the coin has already been tossed and the outcome concealed, people will offer lower amounts when asked for bets. People act as if their involvement will somehow affect the outcome of the toss.[2] In this case, the idea of control over the outcome is clearly an illusion.

The key attributes that foster the illusion of control are choice, outcome sequence, task familiarity, information, and active involvement.[3] Investors may routinely experience these attributes.

Choice. The choice attribute refers to the mistaken feeling that an active choice induces control. Consider your local lottery game. People who choose their own lottery numbers feel they have a better chance of winning than people that have numbers randomly given to them. In the past, most investors used full-service brokers who advised them and helped them make investment choices. However, the rise of the no-advice discount broker shifted the decision making more to the investor. Modern investors must make their own choices as to what (and when) to buy and sell. The more active the investor is in the decision making, the higher the illusion of control.

Outcome Sequence. The way in which an outcome occurs affects the illusion of control. Positive outcomes that occur early give the person a greater illusion of control than early negative outcomes. Even something as simple and transparent as being right on the first two tosses of a coin can lead to an increased feeling of having the ability to predict the next toss. I illustrated the effect of the extended bull market on new investors earlier.

Task Familiarity. The more familiar people are with a task, the more they feel in control of the task. Investing has become a very familiar thing in our society. Consider these indicators:

- In 2000, CNBC (a financial news TV channel) surpassed CNN as the most watched cable news network.
- There are more mutual funds investing in stocks today than there are publicly traded companies to invest in.
- Terms like 401(k) and day trader are household terms.

Information. The greater the amount of information obtained, the greater the illusion of control. When learning new information, people place too much emphasis on how extreme or important it is. Too little emphasis is placed on validity or accuracy. Much of the information received is really noise and is not important—a lot of what we call information is inaccurate, hearsay, or simply outdated. In fact, some "information" used by investors these days is really an *info bomb*—a deception perpetrated by modern scam artists, an issue we'll discuss further in Section 5, "Investing and the Internet." As illustrated earlier, information does not necessarily lead to knowledge or understanding.

Active Involvement. The more people participate in a task, the greater their feeling of being in control. People feel like they have a greater chance of winning a coin toss if they flip the coin. Modern investors have high participation in the investment process. Investors using discount brokers must conduct their own investment decision-making process—they must obtain and evaluate information, make trading decisions, and then place the trades. This is surely an example of active involvement.

RECIPE FOR DISASTER?

The attributes psychologists believe contribute to overconfidence are certainly common in our modern investment environment. Indeed, the ingredients for overconfidence by investors may be at their highest levels ever! This overconfidence leads investors to have too much faith in their estimates of stock value and in predictions about the future movement of stock prices. The next chapter illustrates how overconfidence affects investor behavior.

ENDNOTES

1. Arnold C. Cooper, Carolyn Y. Woo, and William C. Dunkelberg, 1988, "Entrepreneurs' Perceived Chances for Success," *Journal of Business Venturing* 3(2): 97–108.

2. E. J. Langer, 1975, "The Illusion of Control," *Journal of Personality and Social Psychology*, 32: 311–28.

3. Paul Presson and Victor Benassi, 1996, "Illusion of Control: A Meta-Analytic Review," *Journal of Social Behavior and Personality* 11(3): 493–510.

3 Overconfidence and Investing

Milestones

- Overconfidence: A Case Study
- Overconfidence and Trade Frequency
- Overconfidence and Risk
- Overconfidence and Experience
- Overconfidence and the Internet
- Summing Up

Investing is a difficult process. You have to gather and analyze information and then make decisions based on that analysis. However, overconfidence causes you first to misinterpret the accuracy of the information and then to overestimate your skill in analyzing it. This can lead to

> **The investor's chief problem—and even his worst enemy—is likely to be himself.**
> **Benjamin Graham**

poor investment decisions, which often manifest themselves as excessive trading, risk taking, and, ultimately, portfolio losses.

OVERCONFIDENCE: A CASE STUDY[1]

The investor mania that took place over Iomega Corporation after its introduction of the Zip drive illustrates how overconfidence can both affect investment behavior and cause market bubbles. Iomega introduced the Zip drive in the spring of 1995. Avid computer users and computer magazines raved about the product. At the same time, Motley Fool—a financial Internet service that was becoming a popular site for online investors—started a bulletin board where investors could exchange ideas, information, and comments about Iomega. The fun had begun.

The early online investors were very computer savvy and loved the Zip drive. Consequently, they loved Iomega. As the conversation about Iomega heated up with the bulletin board postings, so did the Iomega stock price. The price climbed from the split-adjusted price of less than 50¢ a share at the beginning of 1995 to nearly $4 a share by the end of 1995. By this time, the illusion of control had set in.

Consider how the five key attributes that foster the illusion of control (from Chapter 2) were present and may have influenced the Iomega's true believers.

- **Choice.** These investors chose to follow Iomega postings.
- **Outcome sequence.** Most of these true believers experienced a doubling of the stock price during the last half of 1995.
- **Task familiarity.** The more time the true believers spent exchanging opinions on the bulletin board, the more familiar they became with the company.
- **Active involvement.** By reading messages and responding to board postings, Iomega supporters felt they were actively involved in the dissemination of information. By the end of the year 2000, there were over 59,000 messages posted!
- **Information.** With so many messages, much "information" was being exchanged. I use the quotes to reflect the fact that the Iomega supporters (the *true believers*) had a very biased view of what was an important contribution to knowledge.

Information consistent with the true believers' prior beliefs about the greatness of the company was accepted without question. For example, by extrapolating the number of complaint postings about the Zip drive on an America Online site, someone named Charles Park believed that Iomega was selling Zip drives at a rate of 750,000 per year instead of the 500,000 consensus estimate. After his posting, his 50% increase in sales estimate became the new consensus estimate!

While positive news was accepted on the board without validation (even from anonymous posters), negative postings were treated with disdain. People who posted *opinions* that the stock was overvalued were insulted. Even indisputable negative news such as the company reporting the loss of a big contract or competitors gaining market share was discussed so much that the news was twisted into good news. The Iomega true believers heard only the information they thought was consistent with their prior beliefs.

As the true believers expanded the message postings in 1995 and 1996, the stock price continued to climb. These investors were experiencing the attributes of the illusion of control. Did they become overconfident?

The year before these events unfolded, the average monthly volume for Iomega stock was about 20 million shares. During the Iomega mania in 1995 and 1996, volume skyrocketed to an average 200 million shares per month. Some months saw over 500 million shares traded. Two years after the mania, the monthly volume was back down to 35 million. As you can see (and as we will discuss in the next section), overconfident investors trade!

OVERCONFIDENCE AND TRADE FREQUENCY

Overconfidence increases trading because it causes you to be too certain about your opinions, the same way it affected the Iomega true believers. Your investment opinions derive from your beliefs regarding both the accuracy of the information you have obtained and your ability to interpret it. As an overconfident investor, you believe more strongly in your own valuation of a stock and concern yourself less about the beliefs of others.

Gender Differences

Psychologists have found that men are more overconfident than women in tasks perceived to be in the masculine domain. Although the finance industry has been slowly changing in the United States, investing has traditionally been considered a masculine task. Therefore, men will generally be more overconfident about their ability to make investment decisions than women. As a consequence, male investors trade more frequently than female investors—their portfolios will have a higher *turnover*, a term used in the investment community that indicates the percentage of stocks in the portfolio that have changed, or turned over, during the year. For example, if a portfolio had a 50% turnover in a given year, the investor sold half the stocks in the portfolio during that year to purchase new stocks. Similarly, a 200% turnover is equivalent to an investor selling all the stocks in the portfolio to purchase others, then selling those stocks to purchase a third set, all during the same year.

Two financial economists, Brad Barber and Terrance Odean, examined the trading behavior of nearly 38,000 households that took place through a large discount brokerage between 1991 and 1997.[2] They examined the turnover in brokerage accounts owned by men and women, both single and married. They found that single men trade the most. As illustrated in Figure 3.1, single men trade at an annual turnover of 85%. This compares with an annual turnover of 73% for married men (apparently, having a woman in the house makes the man feel less confident). Married and single women have an annual turnover of 53% and 51%, respectively. Note that this is consistent with what psychologists say about men, women, and

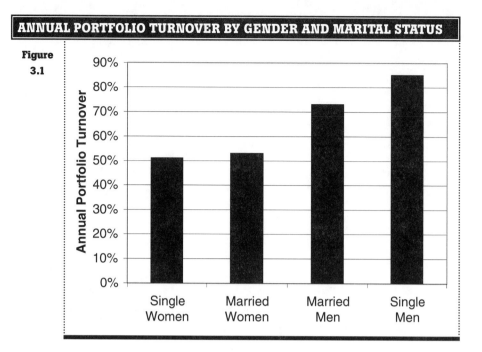

Figure 3.1

overconfidence—that is, men investors are more overconfident than women investors, leading to higher levels of trading.

Trading *Too* Much

Overconfident investors trade more. But is increased trading necessarily bad? If you receive accurate information and have a high ability to interpret it, then your trading should result in high returns due to your skill and the quality of your information. These returns should be high enough to beat a simple buy-and-hold strategy while covering the costs of trading. On the other hand, if you do not have high ability and are suffering a dose of overconfidence, then high degrees of trading will not result in portfolio returns large enough to beat the buy-and-hold strategy and to cover trading costs.

Barber and Odean also explored this issue, examining the relationship between turnover and portfolio returns.[3] First they determined the level of trading for each investor; then they divided the investors into five groups. The 20% of investors having the lowest turnover composed the first group. On average, this group had a turnover of 2.4% per year—basically a buy-and-hold strategy. The next 20% of investors with low (but not the lowest) turnover made up the second group. They continued grouping this way until the investors with the highest turnover were placed into the fifth (and last) group. This last group experienced an average annual turnover of over 250% per year!

Figure 3.2 illustrates the average annual return for each of the five groups. Note that all five groups earn the same 18.7% annually in gross returns—high-turnover investors did not end up picking better stocks for their additional efforts. But the excess trading does have a cost. Commissions must be paid for buying and selling stocks (also illustrated in Figure 3.2). Net returns (returns after commission costs) to the investor are much lower for the high-turnover group. The net returns for the lowest turnover group average 18.5% per year, versus 11.4% for the highest turnover group.

The net difference of 7% per year between the highest and lowest turnover groups is dramatic when we look at a simple example. Let's say you and I both have $10,000 to invest for a period of five years and that I am in the lowest turnover group and you are in the highest. If I earn the 18.5% per year net return for my group, I will have $23,366 after five years of reinvesting my returns. If you, the overconfident investor, receive the 11.4% per year net return for the highest turnover group, you can expect only $17,156—a difference of over $5,000. The difference soars to over $200,000 in a 20-year

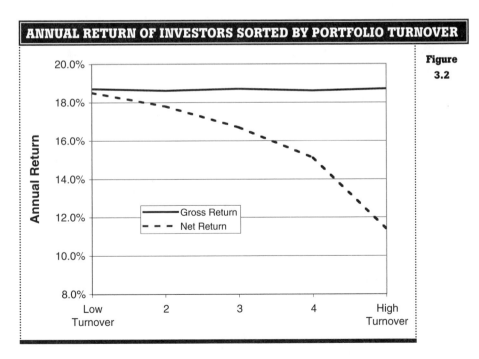

ANNUAL RETURN OF INVESTORS SORTED BY PORTFOLIO TURNOVER

Figure 3.2

period. During my retirement, I will be vacationing in Europe—I'll send you a postcard.

Overconfidence-based trading is truly hazardous to accumulating wealth! One more thing: If men are more overconfident and trade more often than women, do male investors do worse than female investors? On average, the answer is yes. Overall, men earn nearly 1% less per year than women. Single men earn nearly 1.5% less per year than single women. This occurs even though men report having more investment experience than women. It's probably experience learning to be overconfident.

OVERCONFIDENCE AND RISK

Overconfidence also affects risk-taking behavior. Rational investors try to maximize returns while minimizing the amount of risk taken. However, overconfident investors misinterpret the level of risk they take. After all, if you are confident that the stocks you pick will have a high return, then where is the risk?

The portfolios of overconfident investors will have higher risk for two reasons. First is the tendency of overconfident investors to purchase higher risk stocks. Higher risk stocks are generally from smaller and newer companies. The second reason is a tendency to underdiversify the portfolio.

Let's return to the overconfident Iomega true believers. William Bronsteen posted that his entire IRA—A sum worth around $250,000—was invested in Iomega shares. Barry Brewer, another supporter and retired carpenter, invested in Iomega shares with his family to the tune of $2 million.

An entire portfolio invested in the stock of one small company? A person in retirement betting the farm on one small company? Overconfidence can clearly lead to risky behavior!

At the time of these postings, Iomega stock was at a split-adjusted price of about $9 a share. Over the next couple of months, Iomega skyrocketed to $22 a share and then plunged right back to $9. Over the next three years, Iomega rode a roller coaster ride to settle at around $4 a share. Did these overconfident investors get out in time? Unfortunately, psychological biases discussed later (like avoiding regret in Chapter 5) often inhibit you from correcting a mistake.

William and Barry are extreme examples. Your overconfidence probably leads to much less dramatic risk-taking behavior. There are several measures of risk you should consider:

- **Portfolio volatility**—measures the degree of ups and downs the portfolio experiences. High-volatility portfolios exhibit dramatic swings in price and are indicative of underdiversification.

- **Beta**—a variable commonly used in the investment industry to measure the riskiness of a security. It measures the degree a portfolio changes with the stock market. A beta of one indicates that the portfolio closely follows the market. A higher beta indicates that the security has higher risk and will experience more volatility than the stock market in general.

- **Company size**—the smaller the size of the companies in the portfolio, the higher the risk.

The series of studies by Barber and Odean show that overconfident investors take more risk. They found that single men have the highest risk portfolios followed by married men, married women, and single women. Specifically, the portfolios of single men have the highest volatility, highest beta, and include smaller companies. For the five groups of investors sorted by turnover, the high-turnover group invested in stocks of smaller firms with higher betas compared to the stocks of the low-turnover group.

Overall, as an overconfident investor, you perceive your actions to be less risky than generally proves to be the case.

OVERCONFIDENCE AND EXPERIENCE

As discussed in the last chapter, overconfidence is learned. However, it may not take long to learn it. A study administered by the Gallup Organization and designed by PaineWebber Group, Inc., examined the role of experience in investor expectations. The survey was done in 1998 when the stock market was near record highs. They found that new, or inexperienced, investors expected a higher return on their investments than the return expected by much more experienced investors. Additionally, the *inexperienced* investors were *more* confident about their ability to beat the market.[4]

Apparently having been around the block a time or two and having experienced both bull and bear markets help more seasoned investors to unlearn some of the overconfidence.

Mutual Funds

Maybe the solution to this problem is to have professionals invest your money. If you are considering this, remember that professional money managers are people too! They are subject to the same psychological influences as everyone else. Does their education and experience help them overcome the psychological influences of overconfidence?

Unfortunately, this may not be the case. Professional investors can be overconfident too. In fact, psychologists have shown that, in a field in which predicting the future is hard, as it is with investing, experts may be even more prone to overconfidence than novices.

Mutual funds are a good example. During the period from 1962 to 1993, stock mutual funds experienced an average annual turnover of 77%. For the funds delivering the best performance (the highest 10% of all funds) in one year, the turnover rate then increased to 93% the next year. A successful mutual fund begins trading more. Is this overconfidence or is it skill? Apparently it is overconfidence. Having success one year leads to overconfidence. This can be seen by the increase in turnover the next year.

The overconfidence also shows up in the returns. The average fund underperforms the market by 1.8% per year.[5] Mutual funds cannot own too much of a firm (SEC rule). So if the fund has a lot of dollars to invest, it would have to buy larger firms to avoid breaking the SEC rule. These institutional investors also like to purchase risky stocks.[6] Due to the large size of most institutional portfolios, professional money managers are forced to purchase the stock of large companies. However, they tend to pick the large stocks that have higher risk (measured in volatility)—again, a sign of overconfidence.

OVERCONFIDENCE AND THE INTERNET

Thanks to the Internet, "high-quality" information is now easier and quicker to obtain than ever before. However, the Internet investing environment fosters overconfidence. As you acquire more information, your confidence in your ability to predict the future rises far faster than your true ability. Online investors have access to vast quantities of data, but information is not knowledge or wisdom. In fact, having loads of data gives you the illusion of knowledge and thus control. Ultimately, this data may give you a false confidence that you can pick stocks. Indeed, the increase in trading volume in the stock market during the 1990s is often attributed to the rise in popularity of online trading. This has also coincided with the proliferation of online message boards, which seduce investors into the illusion of control.

Due to the illusion of control, investors often become even more overconfident after switching from traditional brokerage trading to online brokerage accounts. Barber and Odean studied the behavior of 1,607 investors who switched from phone-based trading to online trading.[7] Even before going online, these investors were active traders—their average annual turnover was 70%. After the switch to online trading, their turnover increased to 120% annually. Was this extra trading fruitful? Before the switch, these investors performed well. Their portfolio returns (after costs) exceeded that of the major indices (like the S&P 500 index). After the switch to online trading, these investors began *underperforming* these indices. In short, it appears that they became more overconfident after switching to online trading accounts. This overconfidence led to excessive trading and lower profits (see Section 4 of this book for further discussion of these issues).

SUMMING UP

Both individual and professional investors can be overconfident about their abilities, knowledge, and future prospects. Overconfidence leads to excessive trading that can lower portfolio returns. Overconfidence also leads to greater risk taking. You may be accepting more risk due to underdiversification and a focus on investing in small companies with higher betas. Finally, investors' ever increasing use of online brokerage accounts is making them more overconfident than ever before.

Indeed, trading in the U.S. stock market seems overly high. The average dollar amount of the stock traded on *just* the New York Stock Exchange in one year is roughly equivalent to one-quarter of the world's total annual economic trade and investment flow.

ENDNOTES

1. For details on the Iomega events, see Joseph Nocera, 1996, "Investing in a Fool's Paradise." *Fortune*, April 15: 86–94.

2. Brad Barber and Terrance Odean, 2000, "Boys Will Be Boys: Gender, Overconfidence, and Common Stock Investment," *Quarterly Journal of Economics*, forthcoming.

3. Brad Barber and Terrance Odean, 2000, "Trading Is Hazardous to Your Wealth: The Common Stock Investment Performance of Individual Investors," *Journal of Finance* 55: 773–806.

4. Greg Ip, 1998, "It's Official: Stock Market's Pubs Are Likely to Be Bulls," *Wall Street Journal*, July 8.

5. Mark Carhart, 1997, "On Persistence in Mutual Fund Performance," *Journal of Finance* 52: 57–82.

6. Richard Sias, 1996, "Volatility and the Institutional Investor," *Financial Analysts Journal*, March/April: 13–20.

7. Brad Barber and Terrance Odean, 1999, "Online Investors: Do the Slow Die First?" University of California at Davis working paper, December.

4 Status Quo—Or What I Own Is Better!

Milestones

- Endowment Effect
- Status Quo Bias
- Attachment Bias
- Overcoming These Biases

When faced with new options, people often stick with
the status quo. People usually re-elect the incumbent
to another term in office, purchase the same product brands,
and stay in the same job. The desire to keep things the same
permeates all aspects of
our lives. This chapter
discusses how this affects
our attitudes toward
investing. Specifically,
there are three biases involved: the endowment effect, the
status quo bias, and the attachment bias. Here's basically how
they work.

> **Only one thing would be worse than the status quo. And that would be for the status quo to become the norm.**
>
> **Elizabeth Dole, 1999 campaign speech**

- ■ **Endowment effect.** People often demand much
  more to sell an object than they would be willing to
  pay to buy it.
- ■ **Status quo bias.** People have a tendency to keep what
  they have been given instead of exchanging it.
- ■ **Attachment bias.** People can become psychologically
  attached to a security, seeing it through rose-colored
  glasses.

ENDOWMENT EFFECT

Consider a wine connoisseur who buys several bottles of
wine for $5 a bottle and puts it in the cellar. Ten years later
the wine sells for $200 a bottle. What should the wine lover
do? Sell the wine and use the money to buy more bottles of a
less expensive wine? Keep the bottles? Buy more of the same
wine at $200 a bottle? The endowment effect predicts that
the wine lover will keep the bottles because he feels the wine
is worth more than $200 per bottle and yet will not pay that
price to buy more.

What creates this endowment effect? Do we overestimate the value of the objects we own, or does parting with them cause too much pain? Consider the following experiment. Students were asked to rank in order the attractiveness of six prizes. A less attractive prize—a pen—was given to half the students in the class. The other half of the class had a choice between the pen and two chocolate bars. Of those given a choice, only 24% of the students picked the pen. The candy bars were more attractive. Later, the students that were originally given the pen then got to switch to the chocolate bars if they wanted to. Even though most students ranked the chocolate higher than the pen as a prize, 56% of the students endowed with the pen elected not to switch.[1] Judging from this experiment, it appears that you do not overestimate the appeal of the object you own. Rather, you are more affected by the pain associated with giving up the object.

Endowment and Investing

How does this bias affect investors? You will have a tendency to hold onto the investments you already have. Consider that you have just inherited a large sum of money. You can invest the money in different portfolios. Your choices are a moderate-risk company, a high-risk company, U.S. Treasury bills, or municipal bonds. [2]

Researchers have asked people many versions of this question. In some versions, the subjects were told that the inheritance was already invested in the high-risk company. In other versions the inheritance was in the form of the other investment options. *How the inheritance was originally invested was a major factor in the decision of what to do with the money.* The high-risk choice was more popular when the inheritance was already invested in the high-risk company. The Treasury bill option was more popular when the inheritance was already invested in Treasury bills. Clearly the expected risk and return of portfolios dominated by Treasury bills is very different from that of portfolios filled with high-risk companies. Yet the subjects of the studies were influenced more by the status quo than by their own risk and return objectives!

This endowment effect in particular hits home with me. Recently, my wife was given a substantial sum of money by her parents. The gift was given in the form of U.S. savings bonds. As an investment, savings bonds are about as conservative as you can get. They offer very low risk and consequently offer very low returns. My in-laws have enough wealth to meet their retirement needs and are invested in a very conservative manner. My wife and I are in the accumulation phase of our lives with a couple decades remaining until retirement. The investment needs of my in-laws are very different from our needs.

What should my wife do with this money? By the way, my wife has some investment education that comes from participating in an investment club, but she isn't that interested in investing. However, she *does* have an inhouse expert—me!

I suggest, "You should liquidate the savings bonds and buy a fully diversified portfolio of conservative stocks."

She likes the savings bonds.

"Students pay a lot of money to take my undergraduate and graduate courses in investing. In addition to being a finance professor, I am an investment consultant, expert witness, and national speaker," I say, trying to gain credibility.

Her parents gave her those savings bonds.

In short, it was all I could do to convince her to invest half of the gift in stocks. Note that it was not the savings bonds' safety that she valued. She wouldn't put the money into certificates of deposit, a bank savings account, or money market mutual funds either.

STATUS QUO BIAS

The physical sciences would say that an object at rest tends to remain at rest. In decision-making, you often choose the option that allows you to remain at rest. In other words, you prefer the status quo to change.

Consider the plight of a small town in Germany. Due to strip mining of lignite nearby, the law required the government to relocate the town. The government offered to relocate the town to a similar valley close by. Government specialists suggested many alternatives for the layout of the new town. However, the townspeople selected the same layout as the old town, even though the old town's layout had evolved over centuries without any rhyme or reason. The people preferred what they were familiar with to the more efficient and more aesthetic plans.

The status quo bias has a strong impact on employees' contributions and asset allocations in their 401(k) retirement plans (or other defined contribution plan). When you first start working for a new company that offers a 401(k) retirement plan, you must decide how much of your own salary to contribute and where to invest the money. In some firms, you are not eligible to contribute until after one year (or more) of employment.

Consider how the status quo bias can affect your decisions. First, if you are not contributing, then you will probably continue to not contribute. This is very costly. Saving for retirement in a defined contribution plan saves on income taxes and allows for tax-deferred growth of the investments. Furthermore, many employers will match your contribution up to a certain point. If you don't contribute, you miss out on this enormously valuable opportunity. The second way status quo bias affects your decisions involves asset allocation. Your status quo bias will cause you to retain the same asset allocation throughout your working years because you tend never to change your investment choices.

This bias is dramatically illustrated by the experience of a Fortune 500 company that recently changed its 401(k) enrollment policy for new employees.[3] The company's old policy required employees to wait one year after their initial employment date to be eligible to participate in the 401(k); then they had to fill out the paperwork for the contributions to begin. Each employee decided how much of the contribution was to be invested in the money market, stocks, or bonds. The new policy allowed employees to be eligible immediately and automatically enrolled them for a 3% contribution into the money market investment. If employees did not want to contribute, they had to fill out paperwork to unenroll. Similarly, if an employee wanted a different asset allocation than the 100% money market investment, she had to fill out paperwork to make the change.

Under the old policy, one year after becoming eligible for the 401(k) plan, only 37% of those employees were contributing. The new automatic enrollment policy had its desired effect—the contribution rate jumped to 86%. When the old policy was in effect, the status quo bias worked against the employee. Under the new policy, the status quo bias helped the employee save for retirement.

Unfortunately, the new policy had an unintended effect—an asset allocation that was too conservative, a problem also caused by the status quo bias. Since the average age of the employees is in the mid-30s, you would expect the average asset allocation to be tilted toward stocks. Indeed, Figure 4.1 shows that, before the policy change, employees divided their contributions this way: 75% to stocks, 18% to bonds, and 7% to money market investments.

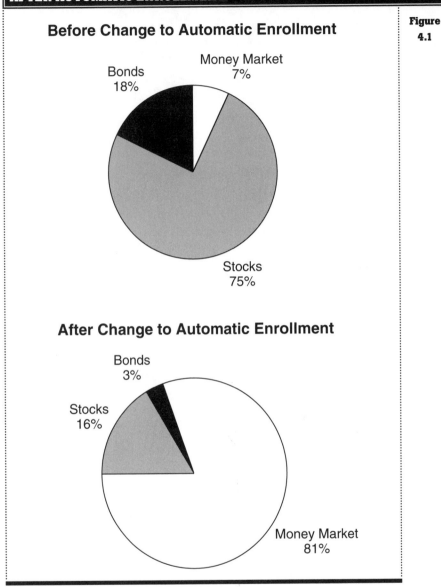

Before Change to Automatic Enrollment

Figure 4.1

Money Market
7%

Bonds
18%

Stocks
75%

After Change to Automatic Enrollment

Bonds
3%

Stocks
16%

Money Market
81%

However, the new policy automatically placed 100% of the contribution into the money market investments. Figure 4.1 also shows how this allocation dominated the contributions of the new employees. When the employee chose the allocation, the mix was 75% stocks and 7% money market. But the automatic allocation led to an average contribution rate of 16% stocks and 81% money market.

Using historical investment data, the asset allocation of the old policy contributors leads to an expected average return of over 10% per year. The new policy contributors can expect just over 5%. The difference will mean that the old policy contributors will have more than double the money in their retirement plans than the new policy contributors will have. The new policy is good in that it uses the status quo bias of employees to get more people contributing to their retirement plans. However, the same bias is causing those employees to invest too conservatively.

The more complicated the decision needed, the more likely you will choose to do nothing. In the investment world, you face the choice of investing in tens of thousands of company stocks, bonds, and mutual funds. Having all of these choices may be overwhelming. As a result, you often choose to avoid making a change. This problem magnifies the asset allocation problem in 401(k) plans. A decade ago, firms offered three or four investment alternatives in the plan. Now, firms offer dozens—even hundreds—of choices. What do you do? Many people do nothing—the status quo.

Your bias toward the status quo increases as the number of investment options increases.

ATTACHMENT BIAS

The attachment bias is similar to the endowment and status quo biases. When you hold and follow a stock for a long period of time, you can get attached to it. This attachment causes you to see the stock through rose-colored glasses. Remember, an investment is *not* a statement of who you are. Stocks are simply a way to increase your wealth. Increasing your wealth is desirable because it can maintain or improve your lifestyle. Figure 4.2 illustrates how investors often lose sight of this.

Consider the client of a financial advisor friend of mine. After a long and successful career working at Procter & Gamble, he retired with a nest egg of $2.5 million. The only problem was that nearly all of it was invested in Procter & Gamble stock. This man definitely has enough money to live an active life in retirement. Any advisor would suggest that first he should switch to a preservation goal instead of a growth goal, and then he should diversify, diversify, diversify.

The advisor could convince him to allocate only a small portion of the portfolio into safer investments when the stock was trading at

**Figure
4.2**

"I want to get married, but I'll be damned if I'm going to sell any Amazon stock to do it."

over $100 a share. In March of 2000, Procter & Gamble stock plummeted to $55 a share. His total retirement portfolio fell nearly 40%. This kind of decrease could change your retirement lifestyle! His response to this event was a desire to buy more Procter & Gamble stock while it was down. Attachment bias can be strong!

OVERCOMING THESE BIASES

How can you overcome the status quo, endowment, and attachment biases? The first step to overcoming them is to recognize that you may be subtly influenced by these problems. Reading this chapter is a good start. However, you should re-examine the investments in your portfolio.

Ask yourself, "If I had only cash, would I use the cash to buy these investments?" If your answer is no, then you are definitely suffering from an endowment or status quo bias. You need to make a change.

Making a change is hard. If it weren't, you wouldn't have a status quo bias. One factor that makes change difficult is your desire to make the right decision. In fact, you may fear making the wrong decision so much that you fail to make any decision. Think about a time when you and some friends wanted to go out to lunch. Does this conversation sound familiar? "Where should we go to lunch?" "I don't know. Where do you want to go?" "What do you think?" The important outcome of this conversation is getting to lunch. Picking the best restaurant is not nearly as important as getting a move on so that you can eat!

You have many investment choices. Which is the best investment? It doesn't matter! For example, consider that you have inherited some money or started to work for a company with a 401(k) plan. You can quickly opt to choose a diversified portfolio that gives you a 10% return. Or you can wait to find an investment that offers 11%. The status quo bias may set in if you wait. It may take you a year to find and get invested in the higher return investment. If so, it will take you over 10 years in the 11% investment, after the delay, to catch up to the accumulation in the 10% investment. Get invested first, and then consider adjustments to perfect the investment later.

It is more important for you to get invested in a diversified portfolio than to spend the time to find the perfect stock or mutual fund.

To be fair, it should also be noted that your status quo and endowment biases might help you in some cases. For example, if you stayed invested in the "old economy" firms and missed the big run-up and subsequent crash of the dotcom stocks, you probably have these biases to thank. Many people did get caught up in the euphoria of the Internet stock bubble.

ENDNOTES

1. George Lowenstein and Daniel Kahneman, 1991, "Explaining the Endowment Effect," Carnegie Mellon University working paper.

2. See the series of experiments done in a university classroom in William Samuelson and Richard Zeckhauser, 1988, "Status Quo Bias in Decision Making," *Journal of Risk and Uncertainty* 1: 7–59.

3. Brigitte Madrian and Dennis Shea, 2000, "The Power of Suggestion: Inertia in 401(k) Participation and Savings Behavior," National Bureau of Economic Research working paper 7682, May.

2

Emotions Rule

5 Seeking Pride and Avoiding Regret

Milestones

- Disposition Effect
- Do We Really Sell Winners?
- Avoiding the Avoiding of Regret
- In Summary

People avoid actions that create regret and seek actions that cause pride. Regret is the emotional pain that comes with realizing that a previous decision has turned out badly. Pride is the emotional joy of realizing that a decision has turned out to be a good decision.

Say you've been playing the lottery.

You have been selecting the same lottery ticket numbers every week for months. Not surprisingly, you have not won. A friend suggests a different set of numbers. Do you change numbers?[1]

Clearly, the likelihood of the old set of numbers winning is the same as the likelihood of the new set of numbers winning. There are two possible sources of regret in this example. Regret may be felt if you stick with the old numbers and the new numbers win, called the *regret of omission* (not taking an action). Alternatively, regret would also be felt if you switch to the new numbers and the old numbers win. The regret of an action you took is the *regret of commission*. In which case would the pain of regret be stronger? The stronger regret is most likely from switching to the new numbers because you have a lot of emotional capital in the old numbers—after all, you have been selecting them for months. A regret of commission is more painful than a regret of omission.

DISPOSITION EFFECT

Avoiding regret and seeking pride affects people's behavior, but how does it affect investment decisions? This is called the *disposition effect*.

Consider the situation in which you wish to invest in a particular stock, Lucent. However, you have no cash and must sell a position in another stock in order to buy the

Lucent shares. You can sell either of two stocks you hold, Microsoft or IBM. IBM has earned a 20% return since you purchased it, while Microsoft has lost 20%. Which stock do you sell? Selling IBM validates your good decision to purchase it in the first place. You enjoy pride at locking in your profit. Selling Microsoft at a loss means realizing that your decision to purchase it was bad. You would feel the pain of regret. The disposition effect predicts that you will sell the winner, IBM. Selling IBM triggers the feeling of pride and avoids the feeling of regret.

Fearing regret and seeking pride causes investors to be <u>predisposed</u> to selling winners too early and riding losers too long.

It's common sense that because of this you may sell your winners more frequently than your losers. Why is this a problem? One reason that this is a problem is because of the U.S. tax code. The taxation of capital gains causes the selling of losers to be the wealth-maximizing strategy. Selling a winner causes the realization of a capital gain and thus the payment of taxes. Those taxes reduce your profit. Selling the losers gives you a chance to reduce your taxes, thus decreasing the amount of the loss. Reconsider the IBM/Microsoft example and assume that capital gains are taxed at the 20% rate. If your positions in Microsoft and IBM are each valued at $1,000, then the original purchase price of IBM must have been $833 to have earned a 20% return. Likewise, the purchase price of Microsoft must have been $1,250 to have experienced a 20% loss. Table 5.1 shows which stock would be more advantageous to sell when you look at the total picture.

If you sell IBM, you receive $1,000, but you pay taxes of $33, so your net gain is $967. Alternatively, you could sell Microsoft and receive $1,000, plus gain a tax credit of $50 to be used against other capital gains in your portfolio; so your net gain is $1,050. If the tax

SELLING TO MAXIMIZE WEALTH

Table 5.1

	IBM	Microsoft
Sale proceeds	$ 1,000	$ 1,000
Tax basis	$ 833	$ 1,250
Taxable gain (loss)	$ 177	($ 250)
Tax (credit) at 20%	$ 33	($ 50)
After-tax proceeds	$ 967	$ 1,050

rate is higher than 20% (as in the case of gains realized within one year of the stock purchase), then the advantage of selling the loser is even greater. The disposition effect predicts the selling of winners. However, it is the selling of losers that is the wealth-maximizing strategy!

This is not a recommendation to sell a stock as soon as it goes down in price—stock prices do frequently fluctuate. Instead, the disposition effect refers to hanging on to stocks that have fallen during the past six or nine months, when you really should be considering selling them. This is a psychological bias that affects you over a fairly long period of time. We'll discuss a similar, but opposite behavior in the next chapter, one that happens very quickly—where there is a quick drop in price and the "snake-bit" investor dumps the stocks quickly.

DO WE REALLY SELL WINNERS?

So, do you behave in a rational manner and predominately sell losers, or are you affected by your psychology and have a tendency to sell your winners? Several studies provide insight into what investors really do.

One study examined 75,000 round-trip trades of a national brokerage house.[2] A round-trip trade is a stock purchase followed later by the sale of the stock. Which stocks did investors sell—the winners or the losers? The study examined the length of time the stock was held and the return that was received. Are investors quick to close out a position when it has taken a loss or when it has a gain? Figure 5.1 shows the average annualized return for positions held 0–30 days, 31–182 days, 183–365 days, and over 365 days. Figure 5.1 indicates that investors are quick to realize their gains. The average annualized return for stocks purchased and then sold within the first 30 days was 45%. The returns for stocks held 31–182 days, 183–365 days, and over 365 days were 7.8%, 5.1%, and 4.5%, respectively.

It is apparent that investors are quick to sell winners. If you buy a stock and it quickly jumps in price, you become tempted to sell it and lock in the profit. You can now go out and seek pride by telling your neighbors about your quick profit. On the other hand, if you buy a stock and it goes down in price, you wait. Later, if it goes back up, you may sell or wait longer. However, selling the winner creates tax payments!

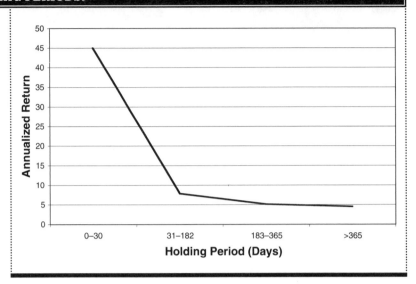

Figure 5.1

ANNUALIZED RETURN FOR DIFFERENT INVESTOR HOLDING PERIODS.

This behavior can be seen after initial public offering (IPO) shares hit the market. Shares of the IPO are first sold to the clients of the investment banks and brokerage firms helping the company go public. As we will discuss in detail in the next chapter, the price paid by these initial shareholders is often substantially less than the initial sales price of the stock on the stock exchange. These original shareholders often quickly sell the stock on the stock market for a quick profit—so often, in fact, that it has a special name: flipping IPOs. There are times, however, that the IPO does not start trading at a higher price on the stock exchange. Sometimes the price falls. The volume of shares traded is lower for these declining-price IPOs than for the increasing-price IPOs. The original investors are quick to flip increasing-price IPOs, but they tend to hold the declining-price IPOs hoping for a rebound.

Another study by Terrance Odean examined the trades of 10,000 accounts from a nationwide discount brokerage.[3] He found that, when investors sell winners, the sale represents 23% of the total gains of the investor's portfolio. In other words, investors sell the big winners—one stock representing one quarter of the profits. He also found that, on average, investors are 50% more likely to sell a winner than a loser. Investors are prone to letting their losses ride.

Do you avoid selling losers? If you hear yourself in any of the following comments, you hold on to losers.

- If this stock would only get back to what I paid for it, I would sell it.
- The stock price has dropped so much, I can't sell it now!
- I will hold this stock because it can't possibly fall any farther.

Sound familiar? Many investors will not sell anything at a loss because they don't want to give up the hope of making their money back. Meanwhile, they could be making money somewhere else.

Selling Winners Too Soon and Holding Losers Too Long

Not only does the disposition effect predict the selling of winners, it also suggests that the winners are sold *too soon* and the losers are held *too long*!

What does selling too soon or holding too long imply? Selling a winner too soon suggests that it would have continued to perform well for you if you had not sold it. Holding losers too long suggests that your stocks with price declines will continue to perform poorly and will not rebound with the speed you hope for.

Do investors sell winners too soon and hold losers too long, as suggested by the disposition effect? Odean's study found that, when an investor sold a winner stock, the stock beat the market during the next year by an average of 2.35%.[4] In other words, it continued to perform pretty well. During this same year, the loser stocks that the investor kept underperformed the market by –1.06%. In short, you tend to sell the stock that ends up providing a high return and keep the stock that provides a lower return.

So we've seen that the fear of regret and the seeking of pride hurts your wealth in two ways:

- You are paying more in taxes because of the disposition to sell winners instead of losers.
- You earn a lower return on your portfolio because you sell the winners too early and hold on to poorly performing stocks that continue to perform poorly.

The Disposition Effect and the Media

Active investors follow the economic and financial news very closely. Given your disposition to sell winners and hold losers, how do you react to a news story? Buy, sell, hold? I examined the trades of individual investors with holdings in 144 New York Stock Exchange companies in relation to news reports.[5] I specifically studied investor reaction either to news about the company or to news about the economy. News about a company mostly affects the price of just that company's stock, whereas economic news affects the stock prices of all companies. The results are interesting. Good news about a company resulting in an increase in the stock price induces investors to sell (selling winners). Bad news about a company does not induce investors to sell (holding losers). This is consistent with avoiding regret and seeking pride.

However, news about the economy does not induce investor trading. Although good economic news increases stock prices and bad economic news lowers stock prices, this does not cause individual investors to sell. In fact, investors are less likely than usual to sell winners after good economic news. Investor reaction to economic news is not consistent with the disposition effect.

This illustrates an interesting characteristic of regret. After taking a stock loss, investors feel stronger regret if the loss can be tied to their own decision. However, if the investor can attribute the loss to things out of his or her control, then the feeling of regret is weaker. For example, if the stock you hold declines in price when the stock market itself is advancing, then you have made a bad choice and regret is strong. In this case, you would avoid selling the stock because you want to avoid the strong regret feelings. Alternatively, if the stock you hold drops in price during a general market decline, then this is divine intervention and out of your control. The feeling of regret is weak and you may be more inclined to sell.

In the case of news about a company, your actions are consistent with the disposition effect because the feeling of regret is strong. In the case of economic news, you have a weaker feeling of regret because the outcome is considered out of your control. This leads to actions that are not consistent with the predictions of the disposition effect.

AVOIDING THE AVOIDING OF REGRET

Avoiding the emotional pain of regret causes you to sell winners too soon and hold on to losers too long. This causes a loss of wealth from taxes and a bias toward holding stocks that perform poorly.

How can you avoid this pitfall? The first step is to understand this psychological bias. This chapter should help you accomplish this step. Two other steps are helpful:

1. Make sell decisions before you are emotionally tied to the position.

2. Keep a reminder of the avoiding regret problem.

For example, when buying a stock for $100, you should decide at which price you will sell the stock if the price declines. You may decide to sell if the price falls to $90. However, making this decision before the price actually falls is not enough. You must act. You must act in advance, before the stock actually falls **The cost of avoiding emotional pain is financial pain.** and regret starts to take place. How do you accomplish this? Place a stop-loss order. A stop-loss order is an order that tells the brokerage to sell the stock if it ever falls to a predetermined price. A stop-loss order at $90 will cause the stock to automatically be sold if the price falls to $90. This order is placed when the stock is still at $100 and regret has not had a chance to occur.

Another strategy is to make a point of selling enough losers to offset any gains that you might have incurred during the year. Although this can be done any time during the year, you probably feel most comfortable doing this in December. In fact, December is the most common month to take losses for tax purposes. Investors often use the end-of-the-year tax deadline as motivation to sell losers. However, losers can be sold at any time during the year to achieve the tax benefits. The reason that tax-loss selling usually occurs in December is that the closer you get to the end of the year, the tax-reduction motive has more influence over investors than the disposition effect.

Finally, keep a reminder of the avoiding regret problem. Consider how many futures traders train to do their jobs. Futures traders often take very risky short-term positions in the market. They can gain or lose large sums of money in minutes or even seconds. Some futures traders have told me that they memorized a saying:

> You have to love to take losses and hate to take gains.

At first, this saying makes no sense. Why would you hate to take gains? The power of the saying is that it exactly counteracts the disposition effect. The avoidance of regret causes traders to want to hold on to losers too long. "You have to love to take losses" reminds them to sell quickly and get out of a bad position when the market has moved against them. Alternatively, the seeking of pride causes traders to sell their winners too soon. "Hate to take gains" reminds them to not be so quick to take a profit. Hold the winning positions longer than your natural desire for pride would suggest.

IN SUMMARY

To summarize this chapter, you act (or fail to act) to seek pride and avoid regret. This behavior causes you to sell your winners too soon and hold your losers too long. This behavior hurts your wealth in two ways. First, you pay more capital gains taxes because you sell winners. Second, you earn a lower return because the winners you sell and no longer have continue to perform well while the losers you still hold continue to perform poorly.

ENDNOTES

1. This example is adapted from Roger G. Clarke, Stock Krase, and Meir Statman, 1994, "Tracking Errors, Regret, and Tactical Asset Allocation," *Journal of Portfolio Management* 20(3): 16–24.

2. Gary G. Schlarbaum, Wilbur G. Lewellen, and Ronald C. Lease, 1978, "Realized Returns on Common Stock Investments: The Experience of Individual Investors," *Journal of Business* 51(2): 299–325.

3. Terrance Odean, 1998, "Are Investors Reluctant to Realize Their Loses?" *Journal of Finance* 53(5): 1775–98.

4. Actually, Odean calculates an abnormal return that is based not on the market, but on the returns of similar firms.

5. John R. Nofsinger, 2000, "The Impact of Public Information on Investors," *Journal of Banking and Finance*, forthcoming.

6 Double or Nothing

Milestones

- House-Money Effect
- Snake-Bite (Risk-Aversion) Effect
- Break-Even Effect
- Would You Buy This IPO?
- The Tech Bubble

Consider this wager on a coin toss: Heads—you win $20; tails—you lose $20. Would you take this gamble?

By the way, you won $100 earlier, and now you are faced with this coin toss wager. Now would you take this gamble? Did your answer change?

What if you had lost $20 earlier? How does the gamble look now?

> A person who has not made peace with his losses is likely to accept gambles that would be unacceptable to him otherwise.
> **Daniel Kahneman and Amos Tversky[1]**

You may gamble in one situation but not in a different situation. The odds of winning the $20 do not change in the different situations. Neither do the risk and the reward. Therefore, it must be *your reaction* to risk and reward that changes between the scenarios.

People seem to use a past outcome as a factor in evaluating a current risky decision. In short, people are willing to take more risk after gains and less risk after losses. To illustrate this behavior, consider the responses of 95 economics students to a series of two-step gambles using real money.[2] In the first step, money was either given to or taken from the student. In the second step, the student was asked whether he or she wished to take the gamble presented. The findings suggest that the students were motivated by one of three biases when it came to answering this question: the house-money effect, the snake-bite (or risk-aversion) effect, and the break-even effect.

HOUSE-MONEY EFFECT

After people have experienced a gain or profit, they are willing to take more risk. Gamblers refer to this feeling as playing with the house's money. After winning a big profit, amateur gamblers don't fully consider the new money as their own. Are you willing to take more risk with your opponent's money or your own money? Since gamblers don't fully integrate their winnings with their own money, they act like they are betting with the casino's money. Professional gamblers probably do not suffer from this bias. One of the characteristics that makes you able to successfully gamble (or trade stocks) for a living is the ability to overcome emotional biases.

You have just won $15. Now you are faced with the opportunity to bet $4.50 on a coin toss. Do you place the bet? Seventy-seven percent of the economics students placed the bet. After just receiving

People are more willing to take financial risk after a windfall profit even when not ordinarily inclined to take risk.

their windfall of $15, most students were willing to take risk. On the other hand, when students were asked to place a bet on a coin toss without receiving the $15, only 41% chose the gamble.

The house-money effect predicts that you are more likely to buy risky stocks after closing out a successful position. That is, after locking in a gain by selling stock at a profit, you are more likely to buy higher risk stocks. Note that this behavior magnifies the overconfidence behavior of Chapters 2 and 3 because overconfident investors trade too much and buy higher risk stocks.

SNAKE-BIT (RISK-AVERSION) EFFECT

After experiencing a financial loss, people become less willing to take risk. This is the snake-bit or risk-aversion effect. When faced with a gamble after already losing money, people generally choose to decline the gamble. Students who initially lost $7.50 were then asked to wager $2.25 on the flip of a coin. This time, the majority (60%) declined the gamble. After losing the initial money, the students may have felt snake bit.

Snakes don't often bite people, but when it occurs the person becomes more cautious.

The snake-bit effect can also affect your investing. New or conservative investors may decide to give the stock market a try. Adding some stocks to a portfolio gives the long-term investor better diversification and higher expected returns. However, if those stocks quickly fall in price, the first-time stock investor may feel snake bit. Consider the young client of financial consultant Norma Mannix, who started by buying shares of a biotechnology company at $30 per share. Three days later the stock fell to $28 and she panicked and sold the stock. Later the stock went up to $75, "but she's afraid to get back in the market."[3]

In the long term, it is harmful to your wealth if being snake bit causes you to avoid the stock market entirely. However, your snake-bit response may be help-ful if it occurs when you are buying IPOs or penny stocks. If these invest-

After having been unlucky enough to lose money, people often feel that they will continue to be unlucky. Therefore, they avoid risk.

ments are not appropriate for you, being snake bit might cause you to avoid them.

BREAK-EVEN EFFECT

Losers don't always avoid risk. People often jump at a chance to make up their losses. After having lost some money, a majority of the students accepted a double-or-nothing toss of the coin. In fact, a majority of the students were willing to accept a double-or-nothing toss of the coin even when they were told the coin was not "fair." That is, students were willing to take risk even though they knew they had less than a 50% chance of winning. The need for breaking even—the break-even effect—appears to be stronger than the snake-bit effect.

Another example of this break-even effect can be seen at the racetrack. After a day of betting on the horses and losing money, gamblers are more likely to bet on long shots.[4] Odds of 15 to 1 mean that a $2 bet would win $30 if the horse wins. Of course, horses with odds of 15 to 1 are unlikely to win. The proportion of money bet on long shots is greater toward the end of the race day than at the beginning of the day. It appears that gamblers are less likely to take this risk at the beginning of the day. However, those gamblers who have won a good deal of money (house-money effect) or who have lost money (break-even effect) during the day are more likely to take this kind of risk. Winners take this risk because they feel like they are playing with the house's money. Losers like the opportunity to break even without risking too much more money. People without significant gains or losses prefer not to take the risk of long shots.

WOULD YOU BUY THIS IPO?

The house-money effect and the snake-bit effect are demonstrated by the demand in 1999 and 2000 for IPOs. IPOs are risky. Many IPOs are companies going public with little sales revenue and significant losses. Because these companies have not been around for very long and have been held by private investors, little information is available. Yet they ask investors to pony up tens, even hundreds of millions of dollars on the expectation that they will grow their revenue and eventually make money. The Securities and Exchange Commission (SEC) recognizes that IPOs are inherently risky and therefore does not allow investors to use margin (borrow money) to buy IPOs.

Investor desire for IPOs is a good measure of how much risk investors are willing to take. Experiencing the big returns in 1998 and 1999 (39.6% and 85.6%, respectively, on the Nasdaq composite), some investors may have felt they were playing with the house's money. If so, investing the gains in these risky IPOs would be consistent with the house-money effect. Indeed, investors seemed to go crazy for IPOs in 1999. Because of the investor demand, a record 548 companies went public.

VerticalNet, Inc., an operator of business-to-business online trade communities, was a typical IPO in 1999. The company reported a loss of $13.6 million on $3.1 million in sales during 1998 and went public on February 11, 1999. Consider these facts about the offering:

- Proposed offer price—$12.00 to $14.00
- Actual offer price—$16.00
- First day opening price—$41.00
- First day closing price—$45.38

Before IPO stock is initially sold, investment bankers for the company making the offering conduct a road show to alert investors of the upcoming sale. The bankers advertise the proposed offer price range and get a sense as to the demand for the issue. If demand is low, they will set the price at the lower end of the range. If the demand is high, the price will be set at the higher end of the range. Setting the final price at $16 when the top end of the proposed range was only $14 is an indication that they felt a strong demand.

Many investors could not buy the shares they wanted from the investment bankers and had to wait to buy the shares on the stock market during the first day of trading. If many investors are forced to buy the stock on the first day of trading, the stock price will rise. If few investors buy during the first day, the price will fall. VerticalNet started trading at $41—a 156% increase from the $16 offer price! A very strong demand indeed.

VerticalNet's experience was repeated throughout 1999 as investors' demand for these high-risk stocks was insatiable. Over half of the IPO firms earned more than a 50% return for the year. Over 50 firms earned more than 500% in 1999!

Just as the great bull market created house money, the worst year ever for the Nasdaq index—especially the tech sector—may have bitten some investors. The Nasdaq composite lost 39% in 2000. The loss was 54% between its peak in March and its low in December. Snake-bit investors recoiled from risky positions. As the snake-bit effect predicts, demand for IPOs dried up. The number of monthly IPOs slowed to a trickle at the end of 2000 (see Figure 6.1)—there were 65 IPOs in August and only 8 in December. Furthermore, there was a change in the type of companies going public. The tech firms with the low sales and big losses were replaced in the IPO market by companies that were already (or nearly) profitable—the IPOs coming to market were less risky than before. Investors who have been snake bit take less risk.

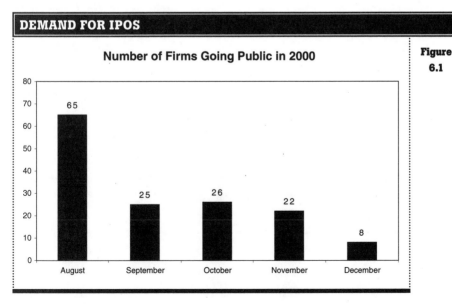

DEMAND FOR IPOS

Number of Firms Going Public in 2000

Figure 6.1

THE TECH BUBBLE

This chapter has been about how you view risk. You tend to seek risk or minimize the effects of risk when you have big gains. Alternatively, you tend to avoid risk or overestimate risk after experiencing big losses. This behavior contributes to stock market bubbles.

The value of a stock derives from its ability to earn profits. The profits from existing operations and the growth of profits in the future are directly related to the company's fundamental value. Companies that generate high profits and growth are valued highly. Of course, future growth is uncertain. Stockholders face the risk of the firm not achieving the expected growth. When companies do not meet expectations, stock prices fall.[5]

Consider two companies. One is considered to have an exceptional management team. The other's management has a terrible reputation. Which is riskier for you to own? Did you pick the company with the exceptional management or the one with the terrible management? Most people think that the badly managed company is riskier. However, this is incorrect. Since people expect the well-managed company to do well, it must perform exceptionally well just to meet those expectations. If its performance is merely very good, it does not meet expectations and the stock price falls. On the other hand, since everyone expects the badly managed company to perform badly, that expectation is certainly not very hard to meet. However, if the company performs just badly (instead of terribly) then it beats expectations and the stock price rises. Therefore, it is not as risky to invest in the badly managed company as it would be to buy stock in the well-managed company. It is not the *level of the expectation* that moves stock prices, but rather the *failure to achieve* those expected profits.

Now let's consider the dramatic rise of the technology and Internet sectors in the late 1990s. The prices of these stocks were driven to incredibly high valuations. The high valuations of e-businesses like Amazon.com, Inc., eBay, Inc., and eToys, Inc., reflected outlandish expectations. Remember, these high expectations also mean high risk. How do you react in a market like this? After watching these stocks experience some good gains, you feel the house-money effect and jump into the market and buy some of these stocks. You either ignore or discount the risks. Even worse, you see the high returns generated by these companies in the past and extrapolate those returns for the future. You think the risk is lower because of the high valuations, not higher!

Eventually, the market valuations get too high to be sustained. The bubble pops. When prices plummet, you feel snake bit. Suddenly risk is important to you. In fact, it becomes the most important factor in investing. You do not buy more of these e-businesses. In fact, you want out—these stocks are now too risky to own! The mass exodus out of the stocks drives the prices down, *too* far in the case of some of the technology and Internet stocks. The expectations of these companies are driven down so low that meeting them should be easy. The risk of these firms is now lower. However, as a snake-bit investor, you overestimate the risk and avoid these stocks.

Of course, you have heard the investment advice, "Buy low, sell high." Why is this so hard to do in practice? One reason is that the house-money effect causes you to seek riskier investments—it makes you buy stocks that have already had substantial increases in price. These stocks are risky because expecta-

The psychological bias of seeking (or ignoring) risk of the house-money effect contributes to creating a price bubble. The psychological bias of avoiding risk in the snake-bite effect leads to driving stock prices too low.

tions have been elevated too much. In short, you buy high. If stock prices fall, you feel snake bit and you want out, so you sell low. The combination of the house-money and snake-bit effects causes you to do the opposite of buying low and selling high. If many investors behave the same way you do, the entire market can be affected.

ENDNOTES

1. Page 287 of Daniel Kahneman and Amos Tversky, 1979, "Prospect Theory: An Analysis of Decisions under Risk," *Econometrica* 47(2): 263–91.

2. This discussion is adapted from Richard Thaler and Eric Johnson, 1990, "Gambling with the House Money and Trying to Break Even: The Effects of Prior Outcomes on Risky Choice," *Management Science* 36(6): 643–60.

3. Tracey Longo, 2000, "Stupid Investor Tricks," *Financial Planning*, April: 116.

4. Daniel Kahneman and Amos Tversky, 1979, "Prospect Theory: An Analysis of Decisions under Risk," *Econometrica* 47(2): 263–91.

5. Aswath Damodaran, 2000, "The Technology Meltdown: Lessons Learned and Unlearned," New York University working paper.

7 Social Aspects of Investing

Milestones

- Sharing Investment Knowledge
- Moving with the Herd
- Speed Is of the Essence (Not)
- Investment Clubs
- Summing Up

Investing has become an integral part of everyday life. Indeed, it has been part of one of the great cultural movements of the century. In 1971 the 10% of U.S. families with the highest income owned 74% of the stock market value.[1] Today, nearly everyone owns stocks. Ownership comes from 401(k) plans, stock ownership plans, mutual funds, and brokerage accounts.

Not only do we own stocks, but we like to talk about them. Investment chatter occurs at the office, over lunch, on the Web, on the radio, at the YMCA—everywhere. Although the 401(k) retirement plan has probably done the most to introduce people to the stock market, it may be the rise of the discount and Internet brokerages that has pushed investment talk into the open. Most people still want someone to talk to about their investments. In the old days, you developed a relationship with your full-service broker. You bought and sold stocks, and you talked. However, you can't chitchat with your online broker. Therefore, you talk to your coworker, your neighbor, a family member, or strangers on your favorite Web site. This has created an interesting paradox. You want to invest on your own, but you also want to come to a consensus with like-minded people.

SHARING INVESTMENT KNOWLEDGE

You want help to "do it yourself." Although this help has moved away from the full-service broker, many other avenues have opened. You can check the consensus of financial analysts on your stock by clicking on your favorite Web site. You can also subscribe to an investment newsletter. There has been a huge growth in these newsletters, as evidenced by the history of the *Hulbert Financial Digest*, a newsletter that reports the recommendations of the other newsletters. It began following 15 newsletters in 1980, and by the mid-1990s the number had swelled to over 90. This is big business—over 2 million subscribers spend $500 million annually on newsletters.[2]

Why all this advice? Let's face it, investing is hard. What price should Amazon.com sell for? If its earnings are one penny off the consensus, what should the price of the stock be? Experts in stock valuation use complicated mathematical models to estimate these answers. But even the experts use price ranges, not exact prices. Why? Because valuation is full of uncertainty.

So, if you cannot compute the value of Amazon.com, then how do you make investment decisions? People that do not use rigorous quantitative criteria in their decision making often get a *feel* for the stock value. This feel comes from investment socialization. What do the analysts say about the stock? What does the newsletter say? What does CNBC say? What does my coworker say? This investment socialization turns other investors' opinions into your "facts," and this is what you base your decisions on.

The popular consensus acts like social pressure. How could all those people be wrong? This causes you to doubt your own judgment when you disagree with them and to have too much confidence in your judgment when you do agree.

MOVING WITH THE HERD

As you learn what other people think about various stocks, the social consensus forms. As you and others act on this consensus, a herd forms. Investor herding is not unlike antelope herding. Antelope stay together in herds for protection against predators. One minute the herd is doing nothing; the next minute the herd is in full gallop. An antelope always has its eyes and ears open so that it knows what other antelope are doing—it doesn't want to be left behind.

The problem with moving with the herd is that it magnifies the psychological biases. It causes you to make decisions that are based on the feel of the herd instead of on the rigor of formal analysis.

You also may be keeping an eye and ear open to what other investors are doing; watching CNBC every day; closely following chat room postings on your favorite Web site; checking your portfolio every day. When things start moving, you know about it. You even may let your friends and coworkers know about it. Do you move with the herd (see Figure 7.1)?

Figure 7.1

"I don't buy stocks simply because others are buying them. I buy them because many, many others are buying them."

Not surprisingly, the feeling of regret that results from picking a loser (Chapter 5) is less severe when you know that many others picked the same loser—misery loves company.

When an antelope sees its herd starting to move, it moves very quickly to join it. This brings up another way in which socialization has had a deleterious effect on the behavior of investors. It stems from the herd mentality and is discussed in the next section.

SPEED IS OF THE ESSENCE (NOT)

The socialization of investing has created an environment where you think you must move quickly in your decision making. If you watch the financial and business news cable channels, you have been bombarded with commercials suggesting that, in investing, the slow die first. You need the fastest Internet provider so you can subscribe to the fastest news provider and trade on the fastest online brokerage system. For a while, CNBC even perpetuated this idea by timing and reporting the responsiveness of the major online brokerages.

Making split-second decisions after news reports in order to move with (or even beat) the herd is not investing. It is trading. Trading is like gambling in that it fosters strong emotional responses. We will explore this in a later chapter that focuses on Internet investors. Unfortunately, this need for speed magnifies your psychological biases.

Consider the simple mistakes that occur when people make split-second decisions. On April 11, 1997, a *Financial Times* story reported that the Czech Value Fund had invested in fraudulent companies and was facing big losses.[3] When the news reached the United States, the stock with ticker symbol CVF fell by 32% on high volume. The problem was that CVF is the ticker for the Castle Convertible Fund, not the Czech Value Fund. By the end of the day Castle had mostly recovered, but that didn't help the investors who sold at the bottom. This is an example of how other investors' errors can cause you problems.

On June 24, 1998, the media reported that AT&T had agreed to purchase Tele-Communications Inc. for $45.8 billion. On that news, the stock with ticker symbol TCI jumped nearly 5% on volume that was more than 37 times the norm for the firm.[4] But TCI is the ticker for Transcontinental Realty Investors Inc., not Tele-Communications. Interestingly, this had happened to TCI five years earlier when Bell Atlantic Corp. announced its intention to buy Tele-Communications.

When you are moving with the herd, you get caught up in the emotions of the moment. When you invest on emotion, you usually end up with poor returns.

This case of mistaken identity occurred repeatedly over a one-year period with people trying to buy MCI Communications in response to a string of takeover rumors. They bought MCI, which is actually the ticker for Massmutual Corporate Investors, a closed-end fund on the New York Stock Exchange. The ticker for MCI Communications is MCIC.

These errors are due to speed. If you buy the wrong stock when it is inflated by investors herding in error, you will lose money. Your emotional high is followed by an emotional and financial low.

INVESTMENT CLUBS

One example of how investing has been socialized is the rapid growth of investment clubs. Investment clubs may consist of family members, friends, or coworkers, for example—frequently all men or all women—who band together to pool their money and invest it in the stock market. These groups typically meet once a month and discuss potential stock investments. Every month the members each contribute some nominal amount ($20 to $100), which is pooled together and invested.

The creation of investment clubs is fostered through the National Association of Investors Corp. (NAIC). Although not all clubs are members of the NAIC, the organization boasted 35,810 clubs and 537,150 total members at the end of 2000. This is a substantial increase from the 7,087 clubs registered in 1990.

Some of this increased popularity comes from the socialization of investing in our culture. Since you discuss your stock picks with your coworker, your family, and your neighbor, it is only natural to form more formal investing groups. However, some of the increased popularity of investment clubs probably comes from the fame of the Beardstown Ladies.

Beardstown Ladies

The Beardstown Ladies is an investment club made up of 14 ladies from Beardstown, Illinois. The ladies, who average 70 years old, became famous when they reported an annual return of 23.4% over a 10-year period. This is outstanding considering the Dow Jones Industrial Average returned 12.1% during the same period. The idea that these adorable ladies could have returned nearly double the return of the market and most mutual funds during this 10-year period gave investors everywhere hope. The ladies became celebrities. They wrote five books on money management, starred in a video, and were invited to give investment speeches all over the country.

Then the famous Beardstown Ladies became infamous. A Price Waterhouse audit reported that their 23.4% annual return was really 9.1%. The ladies actually substantially underperformed the market and most mutual funds. It turns out that they misunderstood the portfolio-tracking software they were using. The higher return seems to have been caused by including new contributions to the portfolio as if they were profits.

Investment Club Performance

The Beardstown Ladies aside, how do most investment clubs perform? The financial press has made frequent claims suggesting that anywhere from 60% to 67% of the investment clubs are beating the market. If true, this figure would also be impressive given that most mutual funds don't routinely beat the market.

However, it is unlikely that these figures accurately reflect the performance of most investment clubs. The claims come from annual surveys of clubs by the NAIC. Consider the problems with this type of survey. First, the clubs have to properly calculate their annualized return. The Beardstown Ladies example shows that this is not necessarily easy. Second, which clubs respond to the survey? If you were the treasurer of a club, when would you respond to a survey by the NAIC? I'll bet you would be far more likely to fill out the survey if your club's returns were very high and avoid filling out the survey if the returns were low. The psychological biases of seeking pride and avoiding regret suggest this behavior (see Chapter 5). Indeed, only 5–10% of the clubs return the NAIC survey. It is very likely that these are the clubs that calculated (hopefully correctly) a high return. Therefore, the survey results represent only the more successful clubs (at best) and are probably totally misrepresentative of all clubs (at worst).

To get a more objective view of investment club performance, the actual stock holdings of 166 investment clubs using a national discount broker were examined over a five-year period.[5] As Figure 7.2 shows, the results are not good. During the period, the S&P 500 index earned an average 18% return annually, but the clubs averaged a gross return of only 17% per year. The return net of expenses was only 14.1%. The clubs substantially underperformed the market. Whereas media reports suggest that more than 60% of the clubs beat the market, it appears that 60% actually underperform the market. Indeed, it appears the same psychological biases are at work in the investing behavior of these clubs as we have discussed in individual investing. Specifically, trading behavior is consistent with overconfidence (Chapters 2 and 3) and the disposition effect (Chapter 5).

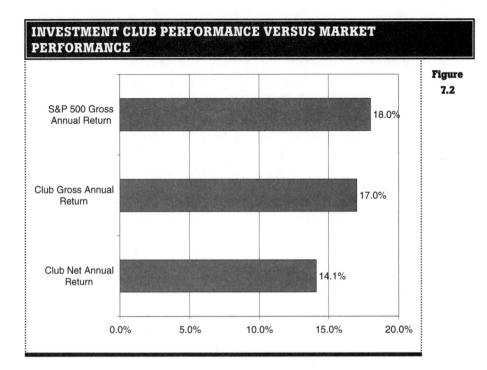

INVESTMENT CLUB PERFORMANCE VERSUS MARKET PERFORMANCE

Figure 7.2

S&P 500 Gross Annual Return — 18.0%

Club Gross Annual Return — 17.0%

Club Net Annual Return — 14.1%

0.0% 5.0% 10.0% 15.0% 20.0%

Investment Clubs and Social Dynamics

Although an investment club's purpose is to create an environment for learning about investing and achieving good returns, most clubs also serve a social purpose. The meetings themselves provide a vehicle for family or friends to regularly meet and socialize. Members like the idea of sharing research skills and knowledge about the market while socializing.

The social dynamics of the club play an important role in its investment success. Some clubs take their stock picking very seriously. For example, the Klondike Investment Club of Buffalo, Wyoming, was rated the number one investment club in America one year by *Value Line*.[6] The 18 members of the club come from all walks of life. Some are young and some are old. Some are blue-collar workers and some are white-collar workers. Some have advanced degrees, while others are business owners. So what is their secret to success? The Klondikers require all investment decisions to be made with the help of a rigorous report produced by the sponsoring member. They rely on research, not just stories about a firm. This is important because the approach helps to avoid some psychological biases. Their decisions are based more on reason and logic than emotion.

Other investment clubs view the social aspects of the club to be the primary objective. Consider the California Investors club founded by a group of retired friends who worked together for many years. Investment decisions are often made without much analysis.[7] Discussions often center on hot tips and speculations. Thus, the club frequently buys at the top and later sells at the bottom and, as a consequence, has earned a poor return. Alternatively, the social events like the Christmas party and a day-long golf outing are planned in great detail. The informality of this club allows each member's psychological biases to combine with those of other members and thus be magnified. The social aspects of the club are more important than the economic aspects.

A high degree of investment formality helps clubs to protect against psychological biases, while low formality magnifies the biases.

SUMMING UP

Section 2 of this book has illustrated how your emotions affect your buy/sell decisions and how you react to winning and losing. I end this section with this chapter because socializing is based on emotional needs. Your natural need to talk to others combines with your interest in investing. When this occurs across a society, we see the socialization of investing.

The next section of the book discusses how your brain functions. Your brain does not work like a computer. You don't process information or remember things like a computer. Sometimes, this can be a problem.

ENDNOTES

1. Marshall E. Blume, Jean Crockett, and Irwin Friend, 1974, "Stockownership in the United States: Characteristics and Trends," *Survey of Current Business* 54: 16–40.

2. Mark Hulbert, 1996, "Mail-Order Portfolios," *Forbes*, February 26: 118.

3. 1997, "Czech Markets Watchdog Chief Forced to Quit," *Financial Times*, April 11: 3.

4. Michael S. Rashes, 2000, "Massively Confused Investors Making Conspicuously Ignorant Choices (MCI-MCIC)," *Journal of Finance*, forthcoming.

5. Brad M. Barber and Terrance Odean, 2000, "Too Many Cooks Spoil the Profits: Investment Club Performance," *Financial Analysts Journal*, January/February: 17–25.

6. Tony Cook, 1996, "Six Moneymaking Lessons You Can Learn from America's Top Investing Club," *Money Magazine* 25(12): 88–93.

7. Brooke Harrington, 2000, "Popular Finance and the Sociology of Investing," Brown University working paper.

3

Functioning of
the Brain

8 Mental Accounting

Milestones

- Mental Budgeting
- Sunk-Cost Effect
- Economic Impact
- Mental Accounting and Investing

Businesses, governments, and even churches use accounting systems to track, separate, and categorize the flow of money. People, on the other hand, use a *mental* accounting system. Imagine that your brain uses a mental accounting system similar to a file cabinet. Each decision, action, and/or outcome is placed in a separate file folder in the file cabinet. The folder contains the costs and benefits associated with a particular decision.

Once an outcome is assigned to a mental folder, it is difficult to view that outcome in any other way. The ramifications of mental accounting are that it influences your decisions in unexpected ways.

Consider the following example:

> Mr. and Mrs. Johnson have saved $15,000 toward their dream vacation home. They hope to buy the home in five years. The money earns 10% in a money market account. They just bought a new car for $11,000 which they financed with a three-year car loan at 15%.[1]

This is a common situation. People have money in savings that earns a low rate of return and yet borrow money at a high interest rate, thus losing money. Mr. and Mrs. Johnson have their vacation home savings earning a 10% rate. Imagine how excited they would be if they found a safe investment earning 15%! But when the 15% opportunity came up, they probably didn't even consider it. If they would have borrowed the $11,000 from their own savings (instead of the bank) and paid themselves a 15% interest rate, the vacation home savings would be over $1,000 higher at the end of the three years.

Money does not come with labels. People put labels on it—there is dirty money, easy money, cheap money, and on and on. Mr. and Mrs. Johnson labeled their savings as "vacation home" in a mental account. Although mixing the "new car" mental account with the "vacation home" account would have maximized their wealth, Mr. and Mrs. Johnson didn't do it.

MENTAL BUDGETING

People use financial budgets both to keep track of and to control their spending. The brain uses mental budgets to associate the benefits of consumption with the costs in each mental account. Consider the pain (or costs) associated with the purchase of goods and services to be similar to that of the pain of financial losses. Similarly, the joy (or benefits) of consuming the goods and services is like the joy of financial gains. Mental budgeting matches the emotional pain to the emotional joy.

Matching Costs to Benefits

People usually prefer a pay-as-you-go payment system because it provides a tight match between the costs and benefits of the purchase. However, things get more complicated when the pay-as-you-go system is not available.

We will look at three questions and how they were answered to illustrate the importance of the timing of payments. Ninety-one visitors to the Phipps Conservatory in Pittsburgh were asked these questions.[2]

> Imagine that, six months from now, you are planning to purchase a clothes washer and dryer for your new residence. The two machines together will cost $1,200. You have two options for financing the washer/dryer:
>
> A. Six monthly payments of $200 each during the six months before the washer and dryer arrive.
>
> B. Six monthly payments of $200 each during the six months beginning after the washer and dryer arrive.

Which option would you choose? Note that the total cost is the same in both options, and that only the timing of the costs is different. Of the 91 people, 84% responded that they preferred the postponed payment option B. This is consistent with the cost/benefit matching of mental budgeting. The benefits of the washer and dryer will be used for a period (hopefully years) after their purchase. Paying the cost over a concurrent period matches the cost to the benefit. Note that option B is also consistent with traditional economics; that is, people should choose B because it allows borrowing at a 0% interest rate.

The next two examples are not consistent with traditional economics. In the next two questions, respondents did not select the wealth-maximizing option. Consider this example:

> Imagine that you are planning a one-week vacation to the Caribbean, six months from now. The vacation will cost $1,200. You have two options for financing the vacation:
>
> A. Six monthly payments of $200 each during the six months before the vacation.
> B. Six monthly payments of $200 each during the six months beginning after you return.

Notice that the payment options are the same as the prior question: six payments before or six payments after the purchase. The difference is that the item being purchased has changed. The main difference is that the benefits of a vacation purchase will be consumed in a short time whereas the benefits of the washer and dryer will be consumed over years. Which payment option would you choose for the vacation?

Sixty percent of the respondents selected option A, the prepaid vacation. In this case, the payment options do not match the consumption of the vacation. The benefits of a vacation are consumed during the vacation. But this vacation must be paid for either before or afterwards.

Traditional economics predicts that people will prefer option B because it is cheaper after considering the interest-free loan. However, most people choose option A. Why? People believe that a prepaid vacation is more pleasurable than one that must be paid for later. The vacation is more pleasurable because the pain of payment is over. If payment is to be made later, the benefits of the vacation are diminished by wondering, "How much is this pleasure costing me?"

An important factor in the decision to prepay or finance is the amount of pleasure expected to be generated by the purchase. The thought of paying for an item over the time that the item is being used reduces the pleasure of using that item. But let's face it, using a washer and dryer is not that much fun anyway. We might as well finance it. The dream home example at the beginning of this chapter is another matter. The pleasure of the dream home should not be tainted with debt and the thoughts of future payments. Therefore, Mr. and Mrs. Johnson are prepaying (saving for) the house.

The third question to the Phipps visitors was different in that it had to do with payments for overtime work. Visitors were asked how they would like to be paid for working a few hours on the weekends during the next six months—before they did the work or after? Prepayment for work to be done was not desirable. Sixty-six of the respondents preferred to get paid after doing the work instead of before. Again, this is not consistent with the traditional view of economics. The wealth-maximizing option is to get paid earlier, not later.

Aversion to Debt

In both the vacation and overtime questions in the previous section, people are expressing an aversion to debt when the good or service is quickly consumed. People seem to have a preference for matching the length of the payments to the length of time the good or service is used. For example, using debt to purchase homes, cars, TVs, etc., is popular because these items are consumed over many years. Using debt and paying off the purchase over time causes a strong match associated with the consumption of those items.

However, people do not like to make payments on a debt for a purchase that has already been consumed. Financing the vacation is undesirable because it imposes a long-term cost on a short-term benefit. This is also true for the third question. People do not want to get prepaid for work because it creates a long-term debt (working weekends for the next six months) for a short-term benefit (getting paid). People prefer to do the work first and then get paid.

This aversion to debt for consumed goods can also explain the surprising popularity of debit cards. Debit cards offer no advantage over credit cards. Credit cards can be paid off every month or the purchases can be carried over to the next month as debt. The cardholder has the option to use debt or not. On the other hand, the purchases on debit cards are paid automatically, like checks. The debit cardholder does not have a choice to use debt or not. The features of a debit card are a subset of the features of a credit card. So why the rapid growth of debit cards? The answer may be that debit cards eliminate the feeling of being in debt and, therefore, allow greater pleasure from the purchases.[3]

SUNK-COST EFFECT

Traditional economics predicts that people will consider the present and future costs and benefits when determining a course of action. Past costs should not be a factor. Contrary to these predictions, people routinely consider historic, nonrecoverable costs when making decisions about the future. This behavior is called the *sunk-cost effect*.[4] The sunk-cost effect is an escalation of commitment and has been defined as the "greater tendency to continue an endeavor once an investment in money, time or effect has been made."[5]

Sunk costs have two important dimensions—size and timing.[6] Consider the following two scenarios:

> A family has tickets to a basketball game and has been anticipating the game for some time. The tickets are worth $40. On the day of the game there is a big snowstorm. Although they can still go to the game, the snowstorm will cause a hassle that reduces the pleasure of watching the game. Is the family more likely to go to the game if they purchased the tickets for $40 or if the tickets were given to them for free?

Most people think the family is more likely to go to the game if they purchased the tickets. You see, the $40 cost of the tickets does not factor into the hassle of the snowstorm or the pleasure derived from the game. Yet people consider the sunk cost in the decision as to whether to go or not. A family that pays for the tickets opens a mental account. If they do not attend the game, they are forced to close the mental account without the benefit of enjoying the game, resulting in a perceived loss. The family wishes to avoid the emotional pain of the loss and, therefore, is more likely to go to the game. If the tickets are free, the account can be closed without a benefit or a cost.

This example illustrates that the size of the sunk cost is an important factor in decision making. In either scenario the family had tickets; however, it was the cost of the tickets ($40 versus $0) that mattered. The next example illustrates that the timing of the sunk cost is also an important component.

> A family has long anticipated going to next week's basketball game. On the day of the game, there is a snowstorm. Is the family more likely to go to the game if they purchased the $40 tickets one year ago or yesterday?

In both cases, the $40 purchase price is a sunk cost. However, does the timing of the sunk cost matter? Yes; the family is more likely to go to the game if they purchased the tickets yesterday than if they purchased the tickets last year. The pain of closing a mental account without a benefit decreases over time. In other words, the negative impact of a sunk cost declines over time.

ECONOMIC IMPACT

The previous examples demonstrate that people are willing to incur monetary costs to facilitate their mental budgeting process. Remember that people tend to prepay for some purchases but that they prefer to get paid after doing work. By accelerating payments and delaying income, they are not taking advantage of the time value of money principles. Traditional economics would predict that people would prefer the opposite—delaying payment and accelerating income to maximize the present value of their wealth.

Mental accounting causes people to want to match their emotional cost with the benefits of a purchase. Their determination frequently leads to costly decisions. Consider the following example:[7]

> Fifty-six MBA students were asked to select a loan to finance the $7,000 cost of a home-remodeling project. The project involved redecorating (new carpet, wallpaper, paint, etc.) and would last four years, when they would have to redecorate again. They had two loans to choose from: a 3-year loan with 12% interest and a 15-year loan with 11% interest. Both loans could be prepaid without penalty.

Note that the long-term loan has a lower interest rate. Additionally, you could convert the 15-year loan into a 3-year loan (that has a lower interest rate!) by merely accelerating the payments. That is, you could calculate the monthly payment needed to pay off the 15-year loan in only 3 years. Because the interest rate on the 15-year loan is lower than on the 3-year loan, the monthly payments would be lower. When asked, 74% of the MBA students preferred the 3-year loan. These students indicated a willingness to incur monetary costs (in the form of a higher interest rate) to make it easier to integrate related costs and benefits. It seems that the students were willing to pay a higher interest rate in order to guarantee that the loan will be paid in only 3 years.

MENTAL ACCOUNTING AND INVESTING

Decision makers tend to place each investment into a separate mental account. Each investment is treated separately and interactions are overlooked. This mental process can adversely affect your wealth in several ways. First, mental accounting exacerbates the disposition effect covered in Chapter 5. Remember, you avoid selling stocks with losses because you do not want to experience the emotional pain of regret. Selling the losing stock closes the mental account, triggering regret.

Consider a wealth-maximizing strategy of conducting a tax swap.[8] When you make a tax swap, you sell a stock with losses and purchase a very similar stock. For example, say you own Northwest Airlines, which has experienced a price decline along with the entire airline industry. You could sell the Northwest stock and purchase United Airlines (UAL). This tax swap allows you to capture the capital loss of Northwest stock to reduce your taxes while staying invested, waiting for the airline industry rebound.

Why isn't the tax swap strategy common? You tend to consider the selling of the loser stock as a closing of that mental account and the buying of the similar stock as an opening of a new mental account. This causes two outcomes that affect you. First, the interaction between these two accounts increases your wealth. Second, the closing of the loser account causes regret. You tend to ignore the interaction between accounts. Therefore, you act to avoid regret instead of to maximize wealth.

Mental budgeting compounds the aversion to selling losers. Consider how you value the timing of payments and benefits. As time passes, the purchase of the stock becomes a sunk cost. The emotional pain of wasting some of the sunk cost on a loser diminishes over time.[9] It may be less emotionally distressing for you to sell the losing stock later as opposed to earlier.

Finally, mental accounting affects your perception of portfolio risks. The next chapter describes how mental accounting leads to the building **The tendency to overlook the interaction between investments causes you to misperceive the risk of adding a security to an existing portfolio.** of portfolios layer by layer. Each layer represents the investment choices to satisfy mental accounts. This process allows investors to meet the goals of each mental account separately.

ENDNOTES

1. Richard Thaler, 1985, "Mental Accounting and Consumer Choice," *Marketing Science* 4(3): 199–214.

2. Drazen Prelec and George Loewenstein, 1998, "The Red and the Black: Mental Accounting of Savings and Debt," *Marketing Science* 17(1): 4–28.

3. Ibid. Discussion is adapted from p. 19.

4. Richard Thaler, 1980, "Toward a Positive Theory of Consumer Choice," *Journal of Economics Behavior and Organization* 1 (March): 39–60.

5. P. 124 of Hal Arkes and Catherine Blumer, 1985, "The Psychology of Sunk Cost," *Organizational Behavior and Human Decision Processes* 35 (February): 124–40.

6. Adapted from John Gourville and Dilip Soman, 1998, "Payment Depreciation: The Behavioral Effects of Temporally Separating Payments from Consumption," *Journal of Consumer Research* 25: 160–74. Copyright Journal of Consumer Research, Inc., 1998. All rights reserved. Permission to reprint granted by The University of Chicago Press.

7. Eric Hirst, Edward Joyce, and Michael Schadewald, 1994, "Mental Accounting and Outcome Contiguity in Consumer-Borrowing Decisions," *Organizational Behavior and Human Decision Processes* 58: 136–52.

8. Adapted from Hersh Shefrin and Meir Statman, 1984, "The Disposition to Sell Winners Too Early and Ride Losers Too Long: Theory and Evidence," *Journal of Finance* 40(3): 777–90.

9. John Gourville and Dilip Soman, 1998, "Payment Depreciation: The Behavioral Effects of Temporally Separating Payments from Consumption," *Journal of Consumer Research* 25: 173.

9 Mental Accounting and Diversification

Milestones

- Mental Accounting and Portfolios
- Risk Perceptions
- Summing Up

The previous chapter detailed how we use mental accounting to track the costs and benefits associated with every decision we make. Mental accounting also affects how we view our investment portfolios.

Fifty years ago, Harry Markowitz, the Nobel prize winner for economics, showed people how to consider all their investments as one whole portfolio. His idea was to own the investments that combine to form a portfolio that offers the highest expected return for the desired level of risk. Combining investments into a portfolio causes you to think in terms of diversification. Investors like the idea of diversification. However, the way in which people implement diversification differs from what Markowitz's portfolio theory suggests.

To implement portfolio theory, you must consider three important characteristics of each potential investment. The first two parameters are the expected return and the level of risk (as measured by standard deviation of returns). Examining the risk and return makes sense to investors. The third important characteristic is the correlation between the returns of each investment. Correlation is how each investment interacts with the others. Mental accounting makes it difficult to implement this important characteristic.

MENTAL ACCOUNTING AND PORTFOLIOS

Stocks often experience large price gains and losses each day—just think about the wild ride of the recent stock market. Modern portfolio theory demonstrates that you can combine different investments to reduce this volatility. By comparing how the prices of different investments change over time, you can construct a portfolio that has a lower risk.

Consider two stocks whose prices move in different price patterns over time. The stocks of Techfirm and Bankfirm in Figure 9.1 have approximately the same return and variation in stock price over time. Both stocks experience large price changes. However, notice that, when Techfirm is advancing, Bankfirm is often declining. Because Techfirm and Bankfirm frequently move in opposite directions, buying both stocks creates a portfolio with reduced risk; that is, the value of your portfolio experiences lower variation over time when you own both stocks than if you own just one.

However, creating a portfolio that reduces risk (in the modern portfolio theory sense) means considering the interaction between different investments. Unfortunately, people treat each investment as a separate mental account and tend to ignore the interaction between mental accounts. Instead, investors build portfolios by making buy decisions on each investment individually. Investors tend to pick investments as if they were picking food at a buffet like the one in Figure 9.2: "This looks interesting … I think I will have some of that … maybe a little of this one … I heard about that one …" The decision to purchase a new security—and open a

The most useful tool in constructing portfolios and reducing risk—the correlation between investments—is difficult for investors to utilize because of mental accounting.[1]

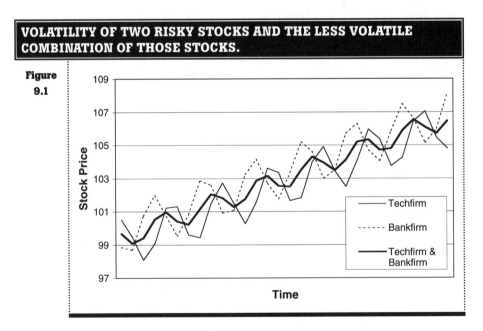

VOLATILITY OF TWO RISKY STOCKS AND THE LESS VOLATILE COMBINATION OF THOSE STOCKS.

Figure 9.1

Stock Price

109
107
105
103
101
99
97

Time

—— Techfirm
----- Bankfirm
—— Techfirm & Bankfirm

MENTAL ACCOUNTING AND DIVERSIFICATION chapter 9

Figure 9.2

new mental account—does not include the investment's price movement with other investments because the mental accounts simply do not interact with each other.

RISK PERCEPTIONS

Viewing each investment as a separate mental account causes you to misperceive risk. You evaluate each potential investment as if it were the only investment you will own. However, you probably already have a portfolio and are considering an investment to add to it. Therefore, the most important considerations for the evaluation are how both the expected risk and the return of the portfolio will change when a new investment is added. In other words, it is how the new investment interacts with the existing portfolio that matters. Unfortunately, you have trouble evaluating the interactions between mental accounts. Consider this problem:

> You have a diversified portfolio of large domestic and international stocks with some fixed income securities. You are examining the following investments:

_____ Commodities

_____ Corporate bonds (high grade)

_____ Emerging markets stocks

_____ Europe and East Asian stocks

_____ High-yield bonds

_____ Real estate

_____ Russell 2000 Growth Index

_____ Small-cap stocks

_____ Treasury bills

How does the addition of each investment change the risk of the existing portfolio?

I asked 45 undergraduate and 27 graduate students taking my investments courses and 16 investment club participants to sort these nine investments by their level of risk contribution to the portfolio. You should take a minute to rank order these investments on their risk contribution to the portfolio. Give the investment that causes the smallest increase (or largest decrease) in risk to the portfolio a 1. Rank the other investments 2 through 9, where 9 is the one causing the largest increase in risk.

Figure 9.3 reports the results of the three groups and shows the standard deviation of returns for each investment. Participants view

INVESTOR'S VIEW OF RISK CONTRIBUTION TO PORTFOLIO.

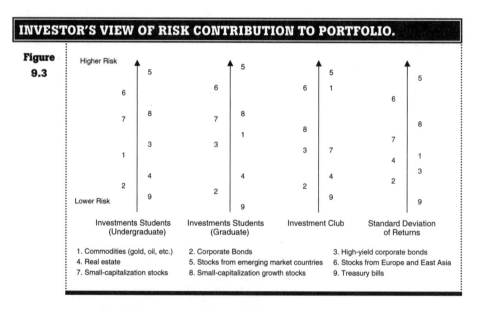

Figure 9.3

1. Commodities (gold, oil, etc.) 2. Corporate Bonds 3. High-yield corporate bonds
4. Real estate 5. Stocks from emerging market countries 6. Stocks from Europe and East Asia
7. Small-capitalization stocks 8. Small-capitalization growth stocks 9. Treasury bills

Treasury bills (T-bills) and corporate bonds as investments that would add the least risk, while they think real estate, commodities, and high-yield bonds would add higher risk. Small-capitalization stocks and foreign stocks cause the highest contribution of risk to the portfolio. Notice that all three groups of participants provide a similar ranking of how each investment contributes risk to the existing portfolio. The last ranking in the figure was calculated using the investments' standard deviation of monthly returns from 1980 to 1997.[2] Standard deviation is a good measure of an investment's risk. The contributions of the three different groups regarding rank order and magnitude of risk are very similar to the risk ranking using standard deviation as the measure. These groups did a good job of understanding the risk of each investment.

However, standard deviation measures the riskiness of each individual investment, not how the risk of the portfolio would change if the investment were added! Doesn't that sound just like what investors do because of mental accounting limita-

It is not just the level of risk for each investment that is important—the other important measure is how each new investment interacts with the existing portfolio.

tions? Remember the earlier example where Techfirm and Bankfirm had the same risk but combined to reduce risk in a portfolio?

Figure 9.4 plots the standard deviation of monthly stock returns for each investment versus the investment's contribution of risk to the existing portfolio, as measured by beta. A beta > 1 indicates that the investment would increase the risk of the portfolio. A beta < 1 indicates that adding the security would reduce the risk of the portfolio.

Notice that the last risk ranking (the standard deviation of returns) in Figure 9.3 is simply the y-axis of Figure 9.4. Because of mental accounting, investors misinterpret the risk of adding investments to their portfolios as the individual risk (standard deviation) of each investment. However, the investment's real contribution to portfolio risk is measured on the x-axis. Figure 9.5 shows just the x-axis from Figure 9.4—the interaction between the investment and the existing portfolio.

Figure 9.5 shows that, if you want to reduce the risk of your portfolio, you should add real estate and commodities. Does this come as a surprise? Figure 9.5 also shows that small-cap stocks and stocks like those in the Russell 2000 Growth Index increase the risk

INVESTMENT RISK AND RISK CONTRIBUTION TO PORTFOLIO.

Figure 9.4

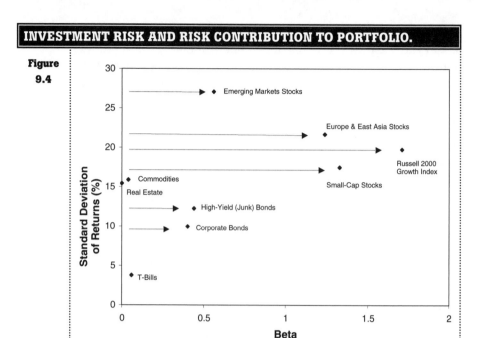

CHANGE IN PORTFOLIO RISK AFTER ADDING THE INVESTMENT.

Figure 9.5

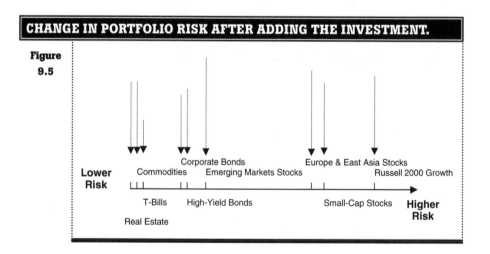

of the portfolio. Viewed by themselves, emerging markets stocks are the most risky investments in the example. However, according to Figure 9.5, they interact with the existing portfolio such that they would actually reduce the risk of the portfolio, if added!

Now let's consider the conservative investor who owns only bonds. This investor owns only bonds because she wants low risk. During the 30-year period 1970–99, her portfolio earned an average annual return of 9.56%. You may not appreciate standard deviation as a measure of risk, so consider these two alternatives: maximum annual loss and number of years with a negative return. The worst annual return during the 1970–99 period was –8.96%, while the portfolio lost money in 9 of the 30 years.[3]

If this conservative investor would add some stocks to her portfolio, she would see the miracle of diversification. A portfolio of 90% bonds and 10% large stocks would have averaged 10.09% per year. It's interesting that the worst return would have been –6.86% and that the portfolio would have lost money in only 7 of the 30 years. Again, this is hard for investors to understand because of mental accounting. The reduction in risk occurs because the prices of stocks and bonds often move in opposite directions. Mental accounting blocks an investor's ability to visualize the various movements of multiple investment categories, all of which can act together for the greater good of the portfolio.

Let's look at another example—the stock and bond markets in 1999 and 2000. If you owned long-term Treasury bonds, your returns were –8.7% in 1999 and 15.0% in 2000. If you think of risk as the chance to lose money, you might think there is a great deal of risk in this type of investment. If you think of risk as big differences in returns from year to year, then you would also conclude that there is risk in Treasury bonds.

The addition of some of the riskier stocks to a conservative, low-risk portfolio of bonds can actually reduce the total risk!

Instead, you probably owned stocks. The S&P 500 index earned 19.5% and –10.2% in 1999 and 2000, respectively. Again, there is a lot of risk here. However, if your portfolio consisted of 50% stocks and 50% bonds, your return would have been 5.4% and 2.4%. Owning both stocks and bonds is less risky than owning just stocks or just bonds. Here is the amazing part: If you owned bonds, your total return for the two years was 5.0%. The two-year return for stocks was 7.3%. If you had 50% stocks and 50% bonds (and rebalanced to this allocation each year), your two-year return would have been 7.9%—higher than owning either just stocks or just bonds!

Modern portfolio theory is clearly an advanced investment topic. Unfortunately, mental accounting makes it a hard topic as well. However, there are several things to remember that will help you implement a diversified portfolio:

- Diversification reduces risk and contributes to higher returns over time.
- Diversification can be implemented by owning many different asset classes.
- Within each asset class, owning a variety of different securities further reduces risk.

Risk Perception in the Real World

Public pension systems demonstrate how the misperception of risk caused by mental accounting affects portfolios. Public pension systems are the retirement plans of public employees such as teachers, police, and state and city employees. The state or local government sets aside money each year to be invested, which is ultimately used as the employees' retirement income. Professional money managers are hired to invest the money, but the government has the power to restrict the managers from investing in specific securities in an attempt to limit the risk of the portfolio. Because of mental accounting, the government officials tend to use each security's individual risk (as shown in Figure 9.4) instead of the interaction risk effect (as shown in Figure 9.5) to make these decisions.

The Government Finance Officers Association surveyed public pension plans in 1999 about the investment restrictions under which they operate. A total of 211 retirement plans responded.[4] Remember that Figure 9.5 showed that real estate, corporate bonds, and even foreign stocks can reduce the risk of a typical portfolio. However, 14 plans responded that they cannot invest in real estate. A total of 8 plans could not invest in corporate bonds, and 19 plans cannot invest in foreign securities. Many more plans have other limitations, such as a maximum investment of no more than 5% of the portfolio in real estate, corporate bonds, and foreign securities. It's interesting that three plans cannot invest in U.S. stocks at all! Those government policy makers need to read this book!

Building Behavioral Portfolios

Investors like the idea of diversification, but they don't build portfolios in a manner suggested by portfolio theory. So how do investors build a diversified portfolio?

Your psychological tendencies cause you to think of your portfolios as a pyramid of assets.[5] Each layer in the pyramid represents

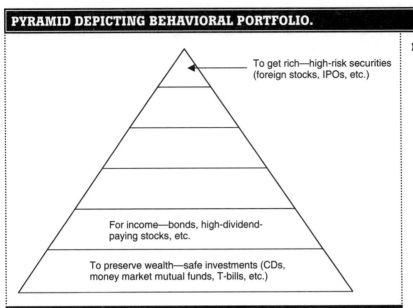

PYRAMID DEPICTING BEHAVIORAL PORTFOLIO.

Figure 9.6

To get rich—high-risk securities (foreign stocks, IPOs, etc.)

For income—bonds, high-dividend-paying stocks, etc.

To preserve wealth—safe investments (CDs, money market mutual funds, T-bills, etc.)

assets intended to meet a particular goal (see the pyramid depicted in Figure 9.6). You have a separate mental account for each investment goal, and you are willing to take different levels of risk for each goal. Thus you select investments for each mental account by finding assets that match the expected return and risk of the mental account.

First, you have a goal of safety. Therefore, you allocate enough assets in the safest layer (bottom of pyramid) to satisfy your mental accounts. Then mental accounts with higher levels of expected return and risk tolerance can be satisfied by allocating assets to the appropriate investments in another layer. For example, investors in retirement have need for investment income. The income goal is met in a layer of the pyramid with assets invested in bonds and high-dividend-paying stocks. After the income goal is met, the retiree may have the goal of keeping up with inflation. This investor would then have a set of assets in a layer that invests for growth.

Each mental account has an amount of money designated for its particular investment goal. The number of mental accounts requiring safety determines the amount of money placed in safe investments. On the other hand, some mental accounts designate "get-rich" assets. In sum, the total asset allocation of your portfolio is determined by how much money is designated for each asset class by your mental accounts. Some investors without many safety-oriented goals will have a greater amount of money placed in high-risk securities. Other investors have many safety or income goals and therefore have more securities in those layers of the pyramid.

The outcome is that portfolios are determined, formed, and changed because of the distribution of investment goals and associated mental accounts. You have a tendency to overlook the interaction between mental accounts and between investment assets. Your diversification comes from investment goal diversification rather than from a purposeful asset diversification as described in Markowitz's portfolio theory.

SUMMING UP

In short, mental accounting causes you to misperceive the risk of individual securities. This leads to the formation of poorly diversified portfolios. As a consequence, you are taking too much risk for the level of expected return you are getting. Or, stated another way, you could obtain higher returns for the level of risk you are taking.

ENDNOTES

1. Roger G. Clarke, Scott Krase, and Meir Statman, 1994, "Tracking Errors, Regret, and Tactical Asset Allocation," *Journal of Portfolio Management* 20(3): 16–24.

2. Data for these figures come from Frank K. Reilly and Keith C. Brown, 2000, *Investment Analysis and Portfolio Management*, Dryden Press, 93, table 3.7.

3. This analysis uses the data compiled by Ibbotson and Associates, 2000, *Stocks, Bonds, Bills, and Inflation 2000 Yearbook.*

4. These results are calculated using the Pendat 2000 Database, which can be purchased from the Government Finance Officers Association.

5. Hersh Shefrin and Meir Statman, 2000, "Behavioral Portfolio Theory," *Journal of Financial and Quantitative Analysis* 35(2): 127–151; Meir Statman, 1999, "Foreign Stocks in Behavioral Portfolios," *Financial Analysts Journal*, March/April: 12–16.

(10) That's Not the Way I Remember It

Milestones

- Memory and Investment Decisions
- Cognitive Dissonance
- Memory and Socialization
- Reference Points
- Summing Up

Memory is not a factual recording of events. Psychologists have determined that memory is instead a perception of a physical and emotional experience. This perception is affected by the way in which the events unfold. The process that records events in the brain can store different features of the experience. These stored features are the basis for subsequent recall.

Memory has an adaptive function: It determines whether a situation experienced in the past should now be desired or avoided. For example, if you remember an experience as having been worse than it really was, you would be excessively motivated to avoid similar experiences. Alternatively, if you remember an experience as better than it was, you will invest too much effort in seeking similar experiences. Therefore, inaccurate perceptions of past experiences can cause you to make poor decisions.

Experiments in psychology illustrate how memory works to affect decision making. Students experienced pain by sticking their right hands in ice water (temperature of 57°F) for 60 seconds.[1] Each student placed the left hand into the water for 90 seconds. However, in this trial, after the first 60 seconds at 57°F, the water temperature was increased to 59°F (unbeknownst to the subjects) for the final 30 seconds. Note that the left hand experienced the same level and duration of pain as the right hand. Then the left hand experienced a 50% lower duration of pain, but pain at a lower level. Which hand experienced more pain? Which experiment (short duration or long duration) would you endure if given the choice?

Seven minutes after dipping the second hand in the ice water, the students were given a choice of which experiment they wanted to repeat. Nearly 70% of the students chose to repeat the long trial! Why did they choose the pain experiment with the longer duration?

The *duration* of experiences has little or no independent effect on the perception, or memory, of the pain experience. The most important factors of the pain experience are the *peak* pain level and the pain level at the *end* of the experience. The memory of the pain seems to be the average of the peak pain level and the final pain level (theory of *remembered utility*).[2]

For the short trial with the students, the peak pain level and the pain level at the end of the experiment were the same. However, because the long trial increased the temperature (decreased the pain) at the end, the end pain level was lower than the peak. Therefore, the average between the two levels was lower in the long trial than in the short trial. Consequently, students remembered the longer trial as less painful even though it started with the exact same level and duration of pain as the short trial but then added 50% more duration at a lower pain level.

In this experiment, a majority of the students chose to repeat a more painful experience because their memory failed to recall an accurate perception of the past experience. In a similar experiment, researchers found that students' memory of the experience changed over time—the farther in the past the pain trials, the less painful the students remembered them to be.[3]

MEMORY AND INVESTMENT DECISIONS

The phenomenon of our perception of past experiences being different from the facts of the experience can affect investors as well. The price pattern of a stock can affect how you make decisions in the future. Say you purchased stock in two companies—a biotechnology corporation and a pharmaceutical company—and that each stock is $100 a share. Throughout the following year, the price of the biotechnology stock slowly declines to $75. The price of the pharmaceutical stock stays at $100 until the very end of the year, when it plunges to $80.

For the year, the biotechnology stock was a worse underperformer than the pharmaceutical stock, but the way in which each stock lost money was quite different. The biotechnology stock experienced a slow and gradual decline (not so emotionally painful), whereas the

In your memory, the large loss at the end of the year is associated with a high degree of emotional pain; your memory of the slow loss, on the other hand, gives you less emotional pain.

pharmaceutical stock experienced a dramatic loss at the end of the year. Even though the biotechnology stock was the poorer performer, the slow loss is less painful for you. Therefore, when making decisions about these stocks for the following year, you may mistakenly be more pessimistic about the better performer than you are about the poorer performer.

This same pattern occurs for pleasurable experiences as well. You feel better about experiences with a high pleasure peak and end. Let's look at a different scenario in which the two stocks had an increase in price instead of a decrease. The biotechnology stock slowly increased to $125 over the year. The pharmaceutical stock rose dramatically to $120 at the end of the year. Your memory of these events causes you to feel better about the pharmaceutical stock even though it did not perform as well.

COGNITIVE DISSONANCE

Psychologists have studied specific consequences of memory problems. Consider that people view themselves as *smart* and *nice*. Evidence that contradicts a person's image of being smart and nice causes two seemingly opposite ideas. The brain is uncomfortable with the poor self-image. Psychologists call this feeling *cognitive dissonance*. To avoid this psychological pain, people tend to ignore, reject, or minimize any information that conflicts with their positive self-image. Evidence that cannot be denied is accommodated by a change in beliefs.

Your beliefs can change to be consistent with your past decisions. You want to feel like you made the right decision. For example, racetrack gamblers were surveyed about the odds of their horse winning. Bettors just leaving the betting window gave the horses they bet on a better chance of winning than bettors standing in line to place their bets.[4] Before placing the bet, you feel more uncertainty about your chances. After placing the bet, your beliefs change to be consistent with your decision.

The avoidance of cognitive dissonance can affect the decision-making process in two ways. First, you can fail to make important decisions because it is too uncomfortable to contemplate the situation. For example, when considering the thought of saving for future retirement, some younger people may conjure an image of a feeble person with low earning power. To avoid the conflict between the good self-image and the contradictory future self-image, they avoid saving entirely. Second, the filtering of new information limits your ability to evaluate and monitor your investment decisions. If you ignore negative information, how are you going to realize that an adjustment to your portfolio is necessary?

Cognitive Dissonance and Investing

Most people seek to reduce psychological pain by adjusting their beliefs about the success of past investment choices. For example, you make a decision to purchase a mutual fund. Over time, performance information about the fund will either validate or put into question the wisdom of picking that fund. To reduce cognitive dissonance, your brain will filter out or reduce the negative information and fixate on the positive information. Therefore, your memory of past performance will be better than actual past performance.

Researchers asked two groups of two questions about the previous year's return on their mutual fund investments to see how close investor recollection came to actual performance.

1. What was your return last year?
2. By how much did you beat the market?[5]

Note that these questions ask about both actual performance and performance relative to the possible alternatives.

What was your return last year? Most people don't remember their exact return. However, if they are not affected by cognitive dissonance, then some will remember the return as lower than the actual return, whereas others will remember it as higher. In a group of investors, the recollections of performance should average out to be near the actual performance.

As I mentioned before, researchers asked two groups of investors these questions. The first group consisted of architects. Architects are highly educated professionals, but they may not be knowledgeable about investing. Twelve architects responded regarding 29 investments they owned through their defined contribution pension plan. Figure 10.1 shows the errors in the architects' memories. On average, they recalled investment performance that was 6.22% higher than their actual return. They thought they did much better than they actually did!

It is very difficult to outperform the market. Most stock mutual funds cannot consistently beat the S&P 500 index. So, by how much

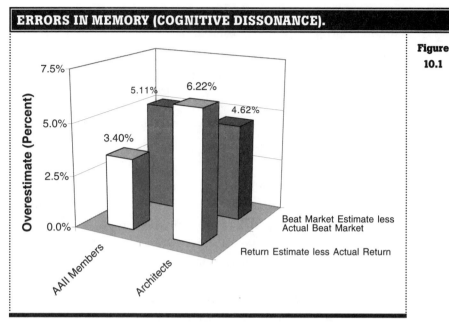

ERRORS IN MEMORY (COGNITIVE DISSONANCE).

Figure
10.1

did the architects think they beat the market (the researcher's second question)? On average, their estimate was 4.62% too optimistic. This group of investors overestimated their actual return *and* overestimated their return relative to a benchmark.

The second group of investors in this research study were members of a state chapter of the American Association of Individual Investors (AAII). The AAII is an association that provides education, information, and services to individual investors, so presumably its members are well educated in investing. Do these investors overestimate their past returns?

> You want to believe that your investment decisions are good. In the face of evidence to the contrary, the brain's defense mechanisms filter out contradictory information and alter the recollection of the investment's performance.

Twenty-nine AAII members responded concerning 57 mutual funds they owned. These investors overestimated their past return by 3.40% on average. They overestimated their performance relative to the market by 5.11%. Even though these people are educated investors, they are overly optimistic in recalling their past returns.

Cognitive Dissonance and the Steadman Funds

Cognitive dissonance might explain the lack of action of 21,000 investors in the Steadman funds—a family of mutual funds with four equity funds.[6] It is known as the Rodney Dangerfield of mutual funds. Consider this from *Barron's:*

> That is the crux of one [of] the great financial mysteries of our time: Who owns the Steadman funds, the family of investment vehicles whose performance, by nearly every measure, over virtually any period imaginable, is easily the worst on the planet, throughout the universe, in any dimension?[7]

A little over the top? Not considering that the Steadman funds rank near or at the bottom of all mutual funds over the past 15-, 10-, and 5-year periods. In the mid-1990s, during one of the strongest bull markets ever, the Steadman funds had actually lost money. Although some of this terrible performance can be attributed to poor stock selection and heavy portfolio turnover, most of it is caused by the fee structure. The annual expenses have ranged from 15% to 25% of assets under management. The average mutual fund expense is 1.4%. With expenses like that, who could expect to earn money?

These facts have been published frequently in the media. In addition, a lawsuit and trouble with the SEC have also made headlines. After receiving all this information, who would still own mutual funds like these? Due to the filtering of the brain to reduce cognitive dissonance, the information may not have gotten through to thousands of shareholders. When asked, shareholders admit to ignoring the fund for long periods of time. Some things are just too painful.

MEMORY AND SOCIALIZATION

Recall the socialization of investing discussed in Chapter 7. You like to talk about your investments. You compare your investments to those of your coworkers, friends, neighbors, and even strangers. Your decisions become based on other investors' opinions. This investment chatter also affects the memory of your past investing experiences.

What people remember about the same event is often different. In a court of law, multiple witnesses to an event will frequently recall details that conflict with each other's accounts. Yet, when you talk about an event with other people, your memory of it will change to be more consistent with the perceptions of the other people. Socialization causes a converging of recalled perceptions within the group. It's interesting that the changes do not necessarily lead to a convergence to reality. In other words, after socialization, the recall of the people in the group can be more faulty than before. This is why witnesses that are going to testify in a trial are not allowed to hear the testimony of other witnesses.

When you participate in investment socialization, you learn what others remember about both the stock market and their own performance. Imagine several people suffering from cognitive dissonance, all trying to ignore bad news and focus on good news. When this happens, you hear a lot of good news and not much bad news. With all this good news, *your* investment performance must have been good as well—at least that is how you'll remember it.

REFERENCE POINTS

The pleasure of achieving gains and the pain of suffering losses are powerful motivators of our behavior. However, it may be difficult to determine whether some investment transactions are considered a profit or a loss. For example, Bob purchases a stock for $50 a share. At the end of the year, the stock is trading for $100. Following good investment principles, Bob re-examines his investment positions at the end of the year in order to record and determine his net worth as well as to monitor the progress he has made toward his financial goals. Six months later, Bob sells the stock for $75 a share. He makes a profit of $25 a share. However, the profit is $25 a share lower than it would have been if he had sold at the end-of-year price. Clearly he has made a profit of $25 a share. However, does Bob feel like he has made a profit or does he feel like he has lost money?

This issue deals with a *reference point*. A reference point is the stock price that we compare to the current stock price. The current stock price is $75. Is the reference point the purchase price of $50 or the end-of-year price of $100? The brain's choice of a reference point is important because it determines whether we feel the pleasure of obtaining a profit or the pain of a loss.

Early investigations into the psychology of investors assumed that the purchase price was the reference point. However, investors monitor and remember their investment performance over the period of a year. If the purchase was made long ago, then investors tend to use a more recently determined reference point.

What recent stock price is used as a reference? Possible recent references are the mean or median price of the past year. Additionally, the 52-week high and low prices are commonly reported in the media.

It appears that the most likely reference point used is the highest price of the previous year. Returning to the example, Bob probably feels like he has lost money because he had moved his reference point to $100 when he recorded that price in his end-of-year evaluation. If Bob feels that way, he may not sell at $75 because he would want to avoid regret (Chapter 5). He may wait until the stock price moves higher again so he can break even (Chapter 6). In your mind, the reference point determines whether a position is at a profit or loss. However, you periodically update your reference point to reflect unrealized profits.

You may use other reference points. Consider the social aspects of investing discussed in Chapter 7. Your reference point may be a comparison with others. As Figure 10.2 suggests, you sometimes think of investing as a competition. How was your return last year? Did you beat the market? Or, maybe more important to you, did you beat your coworkers, neighbors, and relatives?

**Figure
10.2**

"How come Jasper's mutual fund is up twelve per cent and mine's only up eight?"

Investing is not a race. It is a method of achieving financial objectives that lead to a better lifestyle. Of course, that doesn't sound like very much fun.

SUMMING UP

This chapter has illustrated that your memory is more a recording of emotions and feelings of events than a recording of facts. This can cause you to misrecollect the actual events or even ignore information that causes bad feelings. But memory can affect you in other ways as well. Chapter 11 shows how your memory of one event, like an investment, can affect your perception of another.

ENDNOTES

1. Daniel Kahneman et al., 1993, "When More Pain Is Preferred to Less: Adding a Better End," *Psychological Science* 4: 401–5.

2. Daniel Kahneman, Peter Wakker, and Rakesh Sarin, 1997, "Back to Bentham? Explorations of Experienced Utility," *Quarterly Journal of Economics* 112: 375–406.

3. Daniel Read and George Loewenstein, 1999, "Enduring Pain for Money: Decisions Based on the Perception and Memory of Pain," *Journal of Behavioral Decision Making* 12: 1–17.

4. Robert Knox and James Inkster, 1968, "Postdecision Dissonance at Post Time," *Journal of Personality and Social Psychology* 8: 319–23.

5. William Goetzmann and Nadav Peles, 1997, "Cognitive Dissonance and Mutual Fund Investors," *Journal of Financial Research* 20(2): 145–58.

6. Edward Wyatt, 1995, "Silence of the Lambs: At Steadman Funds, Investors—But Not Losers—Are Hard to Find," *Barron's*, January 9: F19–20; Robert McGough and Michael Siconolfi, 1997, "Buy and Fold: Their Money's Fleeing, but Some Investors Just Keep Hanging On," *Wall Street Journal*, June 18: A1.

7. Edward A. Wyatt, "Silence of the Lambs," *Barron's*, January 9: F19. © 1995 by Dow Jones & Co Inc. Reproduced with permission of Dow Jones & Co Inc via Copyright Clearance Center.

11 What I Know Is Better

Milestones

- Representativeness
- Familiarity

Psychological research has shown that the brain uses shortcuts to reduce the complexity of analyzing information. These shortcuts allow the brain to generate an estimate of the answer before fully digesting all the available information. Two examples of shortcuts are known as *representativeness* and *familiarity*. Using these shortcuts allows the brain to organize and quickly process large amounts of information. However, these shortcuts also make it hard for investors to correctly analyze new information and can lead to inaccurate conclusions.

REPRESENTATIVENESS

The brain makes the assumption that things that share similar qualities are quite alike. Representativeness is judgment based on stereotypes. Consider the following question:

> Mary is quiet, studious, and very concerned with social issues. While an undergraduate at Berkeley, she majored in English literature and environmental studies.
>
> Based on this information, which of the following three cases is most probable?
>
> A. Mary is a librarian.
> B. Mary is a librarian and a member of the Sierra Club.
> C. Mary works in the banking industry.

Which answer do you think is most probable? I pose this question to undergraduate investment students, MBA students, and financial advisors. In all three groups, over half the subjects choose answer B—Mary is a librarian and a member of the Sierra Club. People select this answer because being a librarian and a member of the Sierra Club is representative of the type of career a studious person concerned with social issues might pick. However, the question asked which answer is most probable, not which scenario would make Mary the happiest.

Answer A—Mary is a librarian—is a superior answer to B. Being a librarian and a Sierra Club member is also being a librarian—that is, answer B is a subset of answer A. Because answer A includes part of answer B, it is more probable that case A is true. A quarter to a third of the subjects asked usually understand this and choose answer A over answer B.

However, the best answer is actually C—Mary works in the banking industry. There are many more people employed by banks than by libraries. If fact, there are so many more jobs in banking that it is far more probable that Mary works in the banking industry than as a librarian. Because working in the banking industry is not *representative* of the shortcut our brain makes to describe Mary, very few people pick answer C.

Representativeness and Investing

A good company is not necessarily a good investment. Investors tend to think one equals the other. People also make representativeness errors in financial markets. For example, investors often confuse a good company with a good investment. *Good companies* are those that generate strong earnings and have high sales growth and quality management. *Good investments* are stocks that increase in price more than other stocks. Are the stocks of good companies good investments? The answer may be no.[1]

Classifying good stocks as stocks in companies with a history of consistent earnings growth ignores the fact that few companies can sustain the high levels of growth achieved in the past. Nevertheless, the popularity of these firms drives their stock prices even higher. Eventually it becomes apparent that investors have been too optimistic in predicting future growth, and the stock price falls. This is known as *overreaction*.

Consider the performance of stocks typically considered by investors to be growth stocks. Since investors like these companies, we'll call growth stocks *glamor*. And we'll use the term *value stocks* to denote the companies that investors typically consider to be less desirable with minimal growth prospects. Investors consider growth companies to be firms with growing business operations. The average growth rate in sales for all companies over the past five years is a good measure of business growth. The 10% of companies with the highest average growth rates are glamor firms, while the companies with the lowest sales growth are value firms. Glamor or value, which stocks are better investments over the next 12 months? The next five years?

One study uses data for all stocks on both the New York Stock Exchange and the American Stock Exchange over the period 1963–90. The results are shown in Figure 11.1.[2] Say that you identify the glamor stocks in 1963. You buy these stocks and hold them for one year. In 1964, you also identify the glamor stocks. You buy and hold these for one year. By 1990, your glamor stocks investing strategy earned you an average 11.4% return per year. This compares to an average return of 18.7% for a value stock investing strategy. The average total return over a five-year holding period was 81.8% for the glamor stocks and 143.4% for the value stocks. Another popular measure of glamor/value stocks is the price/earnings (P/E) ratio. Companies with high P/E ratios are more glamorous than firms with low P/E ratios. Figure 11.1 also demonstrates that value stocks outperform glamor stocks when the P/E ratio is used to measure performance.

Here is a stock that might interest you—a technology firm that

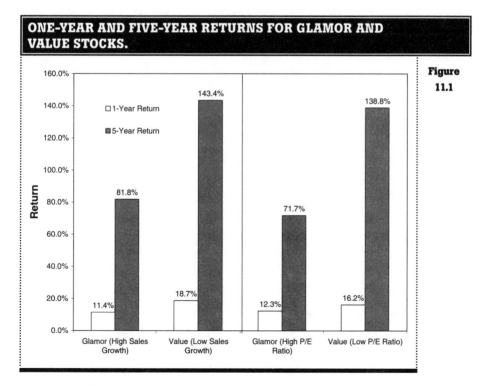

ONE-YEAR AND FIVE-YEAR RETURNS FOR GLAMOR AND VALUE STOCKS.

Figure
11.1

has increased sales by more than 20% per year in the past couple of years and has increased earnings per share by over 35% in each of the past two years. This well-known growth company is no small business—it's Compaq Computer Corp. For the year 2000, Compaq had over $24 billion in revenue and nearly $2 billion in profits. In late 1998 Compaq sounded very glamorous. Indeed, during the three years prior to 1998 the firm's stock had risen 338%. In January of 1999, Compaq stock rose 17% more to $49.25 a share. That was the peak for Compaq. One month later the price was $35 a share. Three months later it was $24. The price eventually fell to less than $20 a share. All this in 1999, the year that may have been the best ever for technology firms.

Good companies do not always make good investments! Investors make the mistake of believing they do because they believe that the past operating performance of a company is representative of its future performance and they ignore information that does not fit into this notion. Good companies do not perform well forever, just as bad companies do not perform poorly forever.

You can make a similar error when examining past stock returns. For example, a stock that has performed badly for the past three to five years is considered a loser. Stocks that have done well for the past three to five years are winners. You may consider this past return to be representative of what you can expect in the future. In general, investors like to chase the winners and buy stocks that have trended upwards in price. However, the losers tend to outperform the winners over the next three years by 30%![3] Mutual fund investors also make this error. The mutual funds listed in magazines and newspapers with the highest recent performance experience a flood of new investors. These investors are chasing the winners.

In short, you interpret the past business operations of a company and the past performance of its stock as representative of future expectations. Unfortunately, businesses tend to revert to the mean over the long term. Fast-growing firms find that competition increases, slowing their rate of growth. Disappointed, you find that the stock does not perform as expected.

FAMILIARITY

People prefer things that are familiar to them. They root for the local sports teams. They like to own stock in the companies they work for.

Their sports teams and employers are familiar to them.

When you are faced with two risky choices, one of which you have some knowledge about and the other of which you have none, you choose the one you know something about. Given two different gambles where the odds of winning are the same, you pick the gamble that you have more experience with. In fact, you will sometimes pick the more familiar gamble even if its odds of winning are lower.

Familiarity Breeds Investment[4]

There are tens of thousands of potential stock and bond investments in the United States. There are also that many choices overseas. So how do investors choose? Do you analyze the expected return and risk of each investment? No, you trade in the securities with which you are familiar. There is comfort in having your money invested in a business that is visible to you.

As an example, consider the breakup of AT&T. In 1984 the government broke up AT&T's local phone service monopoly into seven regional phone companies known as the baby bells. Twelve years after the breakup, who owns these baby bells? It turns out that investors are more likely to own shares in their local phone company than the phone company of another region—they are more comfortable investing in the more familiar company.

The inclination to invest in the familiar causes you to invest far more money inside the borders of your own country than traditional ideas of diversification would recommend. In short, you have a *home bias* because companies from your own country are more familiar to you than foreign companies.

Figure 11.2 illustrates the home bias.[5] The stock market in the United States represents 47.8% of the value of all stocks worldwide. The stock markets in Japan and the United Kingdom represent 26.5% and 13.8%, respectively, of the worldwide stock market. Therefore, to fully diversify a stock portfolio, you should allocate 47.8% of your portfolio to U.S. stocks, 26.5% to Japanese stocks, and 13.8% to U.K. stocks. In fact, modern portfolio theory suggests all investors should have this allocation! But do investors use this allocation? The answer is a resounding no. The stock portfolios of U.S. investors are 93% invested in U.S. stocks, not the 47.8% suggested by portfolio theory. Japanese investors are 98% invested in Japanese stocks. U.K. investors have 82% of their stock portfolios in

DOMESTIC COUNTRY'S PROPORTION OF THE WORLDWIDE STOCK MARKET AND ITS OWNERSHIP BY INVESTORS WITHIN THE COUNTRY.

Figure
11.2

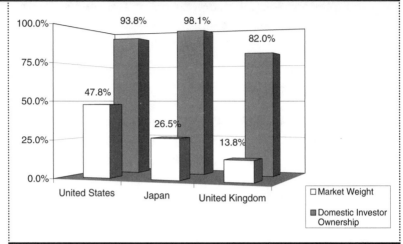

U.K. stocks. Investors purchase the stocks of companies that are familiar to them, and people are simply less familiar with foreign firms.

People invest some, but not much, money in foreign companies. What types of foreign stocks would you buy? Those that are familiar to you. The foreign companies that are most familiar are the large corporations with recognizable products. For example, non-Japanese investors tend to own the large Japanese companies.[6] The smaller Japanese firms that attract non-Japanese investors have high levels of exports. Investors choose stocks that are familiar to them in both domestic and foreign markets.

Americans pick familiar foreign firms, but they bias their portfolios toward U.S. companies. They also tilt their portfolios toward local firms. For example, Coca-Cola's headquarters is located in Atlanta, Georgia. Investors living in Georgia own 16% of Coke,[7] and most of these investors live in Atlanta. Coke sells its products worldwide, but the people most familiar with the company own a large percentage of it.

Professional money managers also invest in the familiar. Even though U.S. professional investors have access to vast information sources and analysis tools, they still tilt their portfolios toward local firms. This is especially true for small local firms and riskier firms.

On average, the companies that a professional money manager buys are headquartered 100 miles closer to the manager's office than the typical U.S. company.[8]

Familiarity Breeds Investment Problems

What company are you most familiar with? Generally, you are most familiar with the company you work for. This familiarity causes employees to invest their pension money in the company stock. For example, most company 401(k) pension plans allow employees to invest money in options like a diversified stock fund, a bond fund, and money market instruments. One common option is the company's stock.

Modern portfolio theory suggests that employees diversify their retirement assets, selecting diversified stock, bond, and money market funds as needed according to their risk tolerance. Selecting the stock of one company is not diversified. Considering that people already have their labor capital tied up in the company, to fully diversify, they should avoid investing their financial capital too.

If your job and your retirement assets depend on one company, you could be in for a shock. Consider the plight of the employees of Color Tile, a Fort Worth, Texas, home decoration retailer. Because the company has declared bankruptcy, many of the 1,362 pension plan participants may lose both their jobs and much of their retirement money—the $20 million pension plan was heavily invested in company stock. The stock of companies declaring bankruptcy frequently becomes nearly worthless in bankruptcy court. Even large established companies can go bankrupt. For example, on April 6, 2001, Pacific Gas and Electric, California's largest utility, filed for bankruptcy.

Your company doesn't have to go bankrupt for you to be adversely affected. Several employees of Miller Brewing Company were going to retire early. Philip Morris owns Miller. Unfortunately, these employees had most of their 401(k) investments in Philip Morris stock. Near the end of 1998, Philip Morris stock peaked at $56 a share. By the end of 1999 the stock had fallen to $23. If these employees has been planning to retire on a nest egg of $500,000, that egg would have shrunk to nearly $200,000. This 59% loss occurred during a time when the general stock market (the S&P 500 index) advanced by 26%. What are the consequences for these employees? Early retirement will probably not be an option. Fortunately, Philip

Morris began a partial rebound in 2000. By year end, the stock had risen to $44.

Just how common is it for employees to invest their retirement money in their company's stock? In a survey of 246 of America's largest companies, 42% of the total 401(k) plan assets were invested in the company stock.[9] Employees themselves make this decision. They like investing in the company stock because it is familiar.

When you are familiar with something, you have a distorted perception of it. Fans of a sports team think their team has a higher chance of winning than those who are not fans of the team. Investors look favorably on investments they are familiar with. They believe that familiar investments will deliver higher returns and that they have less risk than nonfamiliar investments. For example, Americans believe that the next year's U.S. stock market will perform better than the German stock market. Meanwhile, Germans believe their stock market will perform better. Employees believe that the stock of their employer is a safer investment than a diversified stock portfolio.

The brain often uses the familiarity shortcut to evaluate investments. This can cause you to invest too much money in the stocks that are most familiar to you, like your employer's stock. Ultimately, this leads to underdiversification. You allocate too much of your wealth to your employer, local companies, and domestic stocks.

The next part of the book broadens the scope of consideration to the sweeping impact of the arrival of the Internet and how that has magnified your psychological biases.

ENDNOTES

1. Hersh Shefrin, 2000, *Beyond Green and Fear: Understanding Behavioral Finance and the Psychology of Investing*, Boston, Massachusetts: Harvard Business School Press, 81–83; Hersh Shefrin and Meir Statman, 1995, "Making Sense of Beta, Size, and Book-to-Market," *Journal of Portfolio Management:* Winter, 26–34; Michael Solt and Meir Statman, 1989, "Good Companies, Bad Stocks," *Journal of Portfolio Management:* Summer, 39–44.

2. Josef Lakonishok, Andrei Shleifer, and Robert Vishny, 1994, "Contrarian Investment, Extrapolation, and Risk," *Journal of Finance* 48: 1541–78, table 1, panels C and D.

3. Werner De Bondt and Richard Thaler, 1985, "Does the Stock Market Overreact?" *Journal of Finance* 40: 793–808.

4. Much of this discussion is adapted from Gur Huberman, 1999, "Familiarity Breeds Investment," forthcoming, *Review of Financial Studies.*

5. The data for the figure came from Kenneth French and James Poterba, 1991, "Investor Diversification and International Equity Markets," *American Economic Review* 81: 222–26, table 1.

6. Jun-Koo Kang and Rene Stulz, 1997, "Why Is There a Home Bias? An Analysis of Foreign Portfolio Equity Ownership in Japan," *Journal of Financial Economics* 46: 3–28.

7. Nikhil Deogun, 1997, "The Legacy: Roberto Goizueta Led Coca-Cola Stock Surge, and Its Home Prospers," *Wall Street Journal*, October 20.

8. Joshua Coval and Tobias Moskowitz, 1999, "Home Bias at Home: Local Equity Preference in Domestic Portfolios," *Journal of Finance* 54: 2045–73.

9. Ellen Schultz, 1996, "Color Tile Offers Sad Lessons for Investors in 401(k) Plans," *Wall Street Journal*, June 5; Ellen Schultz, 1996, "Workers Put Too Much in Their Employer's Stock," *Wall Street Journal*, September 13.

4

Investing and the Internet

12 The Internet (Psycho) Investor

Milestones

- The Rise of the Internet Investor
- Amplifying Psychological Biases
- Advertising—Increasing the Biases
- Online Trading and Performance
- Day Traders—The Extreme Case
- Summing Up

It is hard to believe that the World Wide Web first began to be mentioned in the news media in 1993 and that the first Web browser became available to the public in 1994. Yet, by the year 2000, there were over 100 million Americans browsing the Internet. The Web's unprecedented growth in users is paralleled by its

> **Using the Internet gives people a sense of mastery of the world.**
> **Robert J. Shiller[1]**

effect on the general economy. Companies like America Online (AOL) and Amazon.com did not exist in 1990; by 2000 they were two of the largest firms in the country. The value of all Internet firms was only $50 billion in 1997, growing to $1.3 trillion in 2000.

The growth of the Internet has changed the way people communicate with each other, shop, conduct business, and receive news and information, and that's just the tip of the iceberg. The Web is also changing the investment landscape.

THE RISE OF THE INTERNET INVESTOR

The Internet has given investors many new advantages. The online investor enjoys lower commissions, greater ease of access, and higher speed of trade executions. No wonder there were 20 million online accounts at the end of 2000. Even investors who don't actually trade online can enjoy increased access to information.

Three different types of companies are providing information on the Web. First, companies that were not originally focused on the finance industry (like Microsoft and Yahoo!) developed investment information services. Second, firms that distributed financial information through traditional distribution channels (like Morningstar and Value Line) began Internet operations. Finally, new investment Internet firms (like Motley Fool and Silicon Investor) were created.

Investment information is also available from the online broker-age firms. Indeed, the ease of access to this information has been a major part of their advertising campaigns. Popular online brokerage firms like E*TRADE and Ameritrade only just started on the Internet in the 1990s, while others (like Schwab Online) were created by traditional brokerage houses.

Many investors like the new tools provided by these Internet firms and Web services. **The speed and ease of using online brokers combined with a powerful bull market made making money by investing appear easy.** In fact, by the end of 1999 there were an esti-mated 5,000 investors actually trading as a full-time job. These investors were dubbed *day traders*. The phrase itself implies that these people are not investing for long-term goals.

AMPLIFYING PSYCHOLOGICAL BIASES

Traditional economics hails the investment advantages created by the Internet as beneficial to you—lower commissions, greater speed and ease of trading, and increased information flow all work to reduce market frictions. A reduction in market frictions improves the marketplace. However, these same attributes magnify your psy-chological biases. The benefits of the Internet are offset by the harm done to you if you are affected by these biases. Psychological biases that are particularly exacerbated by the Internet are the illusion of knowledge and the illusion of control, which lead to overconfidence. Additionally, in Part 2 of this book, emotional factors such as pride, regret, the house money effect, and get-evenitis are magnified.

Information and Control

Using the Internet, you have access to vast quantities of information. This information includes historical data like past prices, returns, and corporate operating performance, as well as current information like real-time news, prices, and volume. Your information access on the Internet is nearly as good as that of professional investors. However, since you probably lack the training and experience of pro-fessional investors, you are therefore less sure how to interpret the information—the information does not give you as much knowl-edge about the situation as you might think.

Many individual investors recognize their limited ability when it comes to interpreting investment information, so they further use the Internet to help them. They get analysts' recommendations, subscribe to expert services, join newsgroups, and learn the opinions of others through chat rooms and Web postings. However, investors must be discriminating when it comes to picking and choosing from this plethora of information. For example, you need to take what you see in these chat rooms with a grain of salt. Not all recommendations are from experts—in fact, most chat postings are from Joe Blow down the street. A recent study examines the stocks recommended in messages posted on two Internet newsgroups.[2] The performance of most of the stocks recommended on the message boards had been very extreme—big gains or losses. The stocks with very good performance the previous month were recommended as a purchase (momentum strategy). These stocks subsequently underperformed the market by 9% over the next month! The stocks that were recommended for purchase with extreme poor performance during the previous month (value strategy) outperformed the market by nearly 9% over the following month. Overall, the stocks recommended for purchase did not perform in a way that was significantly different than the market in general. So, you can see that these recommendations do not contain valuable information. However, if you perceive the messages as having increased your knowledge, you may be overconfident about your investment decisions.

The Internet fosters active involvement by providing the medium for investment chat rooms, message boards, and newsgroups. Internet investment services firms like Yahoo!, Motley Fool, Silicon Investor, and the Raging Bull sponsor message boards on their Web sites for investors to communicate with each other. Yahoo! had message boards for over 8,000 companies in 1998. Users post a message about a company using an alias or simply read the message postings of others.

Consider the messages posted on Yahoo! between December 1, 1997, and July 1, 1998, for 3,478 companies.[3] The average number of postings for these firms was 272. Almost 100 companies had postings in excess of 10,000 total messages. The number of postings on a firm's message board helps to predict the trading volume of the stock the following day. Higher levels of overnight message postings are associated with a higher trading volume the next day. Clearly, many online investors are actively participating in the process, exchanging information, ideas, and opinions in the formation of their trading decisions.

Online Trading and Overconfidence

The illusion of knowledge and the illusion of control are attributes that lead to overconfidence. Chapters 2 and 3 describe overconfidence in detail and show how overconfident investors trade too much and subsequently earn a lower return. If the Internet truly exacerbates the psychological biases that cause overconfidence, it follows then that online investors should trade too much and experience decreased returns. Indeed, it appears that this is the case. For an example of this, lets look at the trading behavior of 1,607 investors who switched from a phone-based trading system to an Internet-based trading system at a discount brokerage firm.[4]

I have already mentioned that portfolio turnover is a measure of how much an investor trades during the year. If you own 10 stocks and sell 5 of them to purchase new stocks during the year, you have a 50% turnover. The higher the turnover, the greater the amount of trading. In the two years prior to our 1,607 investors going online, the average portfolio turnover was about 70%. After going online, the trading of these investors immediately jumped to a turnover of 120%. While some of this increase is transitory, the turnover of these investors is still 90% two years after going online (see Figure 12.1).

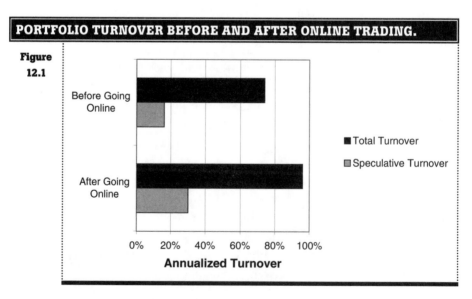

PORTFOLIO TURNOVER BEFORE AND AFTER ONLINE TRADING.

Figure 12.1

However, some of this increased trading, instead of being caused by overconfidence, may result from investors trading to take advantage of liquidity needs or tax-loss selling (see Chapter 5). To investigate trading likely due to overconfidence, the study examines the sales of stocks that resulted in capital gains that are then followed by a stock purchase within three weeks. For example, say you own shares of Cisco and that the stock has doubled in price. If you sell Cisco to buy Intel, you have not traded to change your asset allocation, nor to obtain cash for spending. Instead, you have traded one stock for another. These trades are considered speculative trades. Speculative turnover was 16% two years before going online, and it nearly doubled to 30% two years after going online.

Investors are also turning retirement investments into trading capital. Some firms have given their employees the capability to trade their 401(k) plan assets online. How do the employees/ investors react? They trade. One study investigates the effect of web-based trading in 401(k) pension plans.[5] The advantage of studying these trades is that, since they occur within a qualified pension plan, liquidity needs and tax-loss selling are not factors and thus all trades can be considered speculative. In two companies studied, 100,000 plan participants were given the opportunity to trade their 401(k) assets using an Internet service. The study finds that, after the companies switched to the online service, trading frequency doubled and portfolio turnover increased by 50%.

ADVERTISING—INCREASING THE BIASES

Every day you are bombarded with advertising that magnifies your psychological biases. This is no accident. Financial services firms, online brokerages, and even Internet providers know how to increase your level of excitement.

An E*TRADE commercial claims that online investing is "A cinch. A snap. A piece of cake." A middle-aged woman in a Datek Online commercial declares, "I'm managing my portfolio better than my broker ever did." Two suburban moms return home from jogging in an Ameritrade commercial: a few clicks later one says, "I think I just made about $1,700!"

Consider the infomercial run by "Teach Me to Trade, LLC." Many testimonials describe how the system being sold has allowed them to trade four to five hours a day, even as little as one to two hours a day, and earn $1,700, $2,500, even up to $4,600 in profits per day. Clearly, it must be *easy* to obtain *wealth* by frequently trading. Comments abound like "everyone is trading," "this system is all you need," and "I would rather take control of my investments." Notice how the social aspects, the illusion of information, and the illusion of control are fostered. Unwittingly, the infomercial also gives a peek at the addictive side of trading with testimonials that proclaim to "love the excitement," or "I don't think anything can compare to the rush."

The ads amuse and entice you, but the message is clear—it is _easy_ to attain sudden _wealth_. What do you have to do? _Trade frequently_.

ONLINE TRADING AND PERFORMANCE

So online investors trade. They trade a lot. However, if the advantages of the Internet outweigh the magnified psychological biases, then we should all start trading. What kind of returns do online traders really get? The online trading study also examines the performance of the investors before and after going online. Before switching to the online trading service, these investors were successful. As illustrated in Figure 12.2, these investors earned nearly 18% per year before going online. This represents a return of 2.35% more than the general stock market per year. However, after going online these investors experienced reduced returns. They averaged annual returns of only 12%, which underperformed the market by 3.5%.

The successful performance of these investors before going online may have fostered overconfidence due to the illusion of control (via the outcome sequence). This overconfidence may have caused them to choose the Internet trading service. Unfortunately, the Internet trading environment exacerbates the psychological problems, inducing excessive trading. Ultimately, investor returns are reduced.

DAY TRADERS—THE EXTREME CASE

Although the term *day trader* has emerged as a household phrase, the number of true day traders is quite small. Day traders trade stocks as their full-time job. Although there are no industry numbers available, probably less than 1% of online investors are actually day traders. They trade into large positions temporarily to capture quick

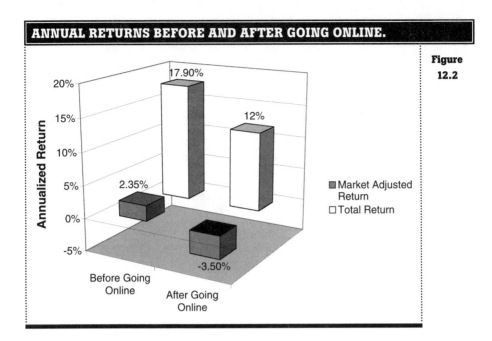

Annualized Return

20%
17.90%
15%
12%
10%
5%
2.35%
0%
-5%
-3.50%

Before Going Online
After Going Online

■ Market Adjusted Return
□ Total Return

profits and then trade out of the positions. Indeed, the average day trader makes 130 transactions in a six-month period. This compares to about 12 trades for the average online investor.

The day trader's tools are a souped up computer and a fast connection to the Internet. These traders may work at a day-trading firm or trade from home. Imagine the attraction of a large screen with multicolored lights. Some lights are flashing indicating a chance to make some money. Add some bells and whistles and you have the Las Vegas casino environment. Indeed, if you are trading at a day-trading firm, then you are near others shouting for joy and anguish. If the Internet environment increases your psychological biases, imagine the amplification in the day-trader environment. Interviews with day traders yield quotes like "it's very addictive" and "you lose sight of everything."

Day-trading firms seem to recognize the psychological problems and the stress associated with day trading. Companies like Broadway Trading LLC offer counseling through a psychotherapy clinic. The nature of day trading is similar to casino gambling. Traders can become addicted. High stress and addiction can cause you to snap.

Consider what happened to Mark Barton. His Atlanta day-trader colleagues described Mark as a nice, religious family man who was having an unlucky streak.[6] (Note the reference to "an unlucky streak"—the idea that profits derive from skill and losses derive from bad luck is a typical psychological bias for an overconfident investor.) Unfortunately, it was much more than an unlucky streak. Like an addicted gambler, Mr. Barton followed big losses with more risk and higher stakes. He could not stop gambling on stocks. Eventually, he had exhausted his money and his credit. Mark Barton snapped. After killing his wife and two children, he showed up at the two day-trading firms he used and killed 6 people and wounded 13 others.

Mr. Barton's case is the most extreme. However, many others feel the same addiction. Consider Gary Korn, a 43-year-old lawyer.[7] He was a day trader in the morning at home, and then went out to practice law in the afternoon. He often made more than 100 trades a day. Mr. Korn describes being mesmerized by the trading screen and hooked on trading. But Mr. Korn is lucky—he recognized his symptoms and quit. After realizing his return over a six-month period was only 28%, he moved his money to a broker. He properly diversified and says he even owns General Motors Corp. stock, although he is "bored to tears" by it.

The day-trading addiction is strong! Mr. Korn may have quit just in time. Not many do. Securities regulators investigating the day-trading firm Block Trading Inc. allege that only 1 of its 68 accounts made money.

SUMMING UP

Overall, the psychological biases induced by online trading and day trading seem to outweigh the advantages. When your focus moves from *investing* to *trading*, your wealth is harmed.

Internet investors don't just risk hurting themselves. Sometimes the frenzy of trading leads to an exuberance that harms the companies being traded. How much of an influence this exuberance has is demonstrated in Chapter 13.

ENDNOTES

1. Page 20, Shiller, Robert J., *Irrational Exuberance*, © 2000 by Robert J. Shiller. Reprinted by permission of Princeton University Press.

2. Michael Dewally, 1999, "Internet Investment Advice: Investing with a Rock of Salt," University of Oklahoma working paper, May.

3. Peter Wysocki, 1999, "Cheap Talk on the Web: The Determinants of Postings on Stock Message Boards," University of Michigan working paper.

4. Brad Barber and Terrance Odean, 1999, "Online Investors: Do the Slow Die First?" University of California at Davis working paper.

5. James Choi, David Laibson, and Andrew Metrick, 2000, "Does the Internet Increase Trading? Evidence from Investor Behavior in 401(k) Plans," National Bureau of Economic Research working paper no. 7878.

6. Evan Thomas and Trent Gegax, 1999, "It's a Bad Trading Day…and It's About to Get Worse," *Newsweek*, August 9: 22–28.

7. Rebecca Buckman and Ruth Simon, 1999, "Day Trading Can Breed Perilous Illusions," *Wall Street Journal*, August 2: C1.

13 Exuberance on (and about) the Net

Milestones

- A Rose.com by Any Other Name
- A Bubble Burst
- The Boiler Room Goes Online

When many investors are influenced by their psychological biases in a common way, the overall market will be affected. This is best illustrated by the most recent investor mania—the irrational exuberance for Internet companies. Many investors and analysts have been puzzled by the extremely high valuations of Internet firms. For example, when the historical average P/E ratio of the market is around 15, what is the justification for Yahoo!'s P/E of 1,300 or eBay's P/E of 3,300 in late 1999? Many analysts concluded that new valuation measures were needed for this new revolution in the economy.

Or consider the valuation of eToys.[1] eToys is an online toy retailer that went public in 1999. Shortly after the IPO, the high price of the stock created a total company value of $8 billion. Typical of Internet companies, eToys had negative earnings of $28.6 million from $30 million in sales. The natural comparison for eToys is Toys "R" Us. Toys "R" Us is the "old economy" leading toy retailer. Even though Toys "R" Us had profits of $376 million, it had a market value of only $6 billion; that is, Toys "R" Us had a lower market valuation than eToys even though it earned 12 times more in *profits* than eToys had in *sales!*

This is even more astounding when you realize that there is a very low barrier to entry for companies getting on the Web. After all, kids started many of the Internet firms on only a shoestring. Indeed, Toys "R" Us quickly developed its own online retail capability and eToys' market capitalization fell from $8 billion to $29 million.

A ROSE.COM BY ANY OTHER NAME

In the immortal words of Federal Reserve Chairman Alan Greenspan, it appears that investors may have gotten "irrationally exuberant" about Internet stocks. Some companies even changed their names to FancyNewName.com. Investors went dotcom crazy and scooped up shares of any company related to the Internet—they could tell which companies were Internet-related by looking at their names.

Look, for example, at the case of Computer Literacy Inc., an online retailer of technology books which customers kept misspelling (or forgetting). Its Internet address was computerliteracy.com, so Computer Literacy Inc. changed its online name to fatbrain.com. Note that this company had already been providing its service over the Internet. The change was in name only, not in business strategy. But when word leaked out about the name change, the online stock discussion groups sizzled and the stock climbed 33% in one day!

From mid-1998 to mid-1999, 147 publicly traded companies changed to new names with a dotcom, dotnet, or the word Internet.[2] During the three weeks after a company's name-change announcement, its stock beat the market by an average of 38%. All kinds of companies got in on the action. Some of them were already pure Internet companies, and these beat the market by 57% three weeks following the name change. Other companies changing names had only some Internet experience—these earned 35% over the market. Companies who were changing their names and also changing their focus from non-Internet to Internet beat the market by 16%. In fact, even companies with little or no Internet experience enjoyed the large stock price increases after changing their names. These firms had a non-Internet core business, and there was no evidence that they had the expertise or experience to be successful on the Internet. Yet, net-crazy traders bid up their stock prices so that they beat the market by 48%, second only to the pure Internet companies! These huge increases in stock prices did not diminish over the following three months. Investors appeared to be eager to throw money at Internet companies. The mania is illustrated in Figure 13.1.

Consider the case of AppNet Systems Inc.[3] AppNet, a private firm, decided to go public and registered with the SEC to conduct an IPO and trade under the symbol APPN. The time between an SEC filing and the actual offering is usually measured in months. Another small company, Appian Technology, was already trading on the over-the-counter (OTC) bulletin board market under the same ticker symbol.

The mania set in. Net-crazed traders touted APPN in chat rooms. Not wanting to miss out on the latest dotcom success story, investors

Figure 13.1

snapped up shares of APPN. Of course, AppNet had not had their IPO yet. The shares that were traded were those of Appian. It is not clear why these traders thought they could buy and sell shares of a stock that had yet to have its IPO. This was not an error made by just a few investors. This was a massive case of mistaken identity. On the day before the AppNet filing went public, Appian experienced a total volume of 200 shares. Yes, you read that correctly—only 200 shares were traded that whole day. During the two days after the filing, over 7.3 million shares of Appian were traded. Also during these two days, the stock of tiny Appian soared 142,757%. Again, you did not read that wrong. It is a statement on how overly exuberant investors were for dotcom companies—that investors would drive up the price so high on the wrong company is impressive.

A BUBBLE BURST

The technology-laden Nasdaq Composite stock index experienced a 54% decline from its peak in March 2000 to its low in December

2000. Internet-focused stock indexes such as the street.com (TSC) Internet Sector Index declined 79% over the same period. In comparison, the Dow Jones Industrial Average actually increased 4%. To put this in perspective, if you had invested $100 in the TSC Internet Sector Index and then lost 79%, you would have $21 left. To get back to $100, you would need to earn a 476% return!

After a market crash, U.S. investors always look to the October 1987 crash for guidance. After a two-day drop of 26%, the stock market recovered in about 15 months. However, the 1987 crash is not the only comparison. Japan ended a decade-long bull market at the end of 1989. The Nikkei Index reached 38,916 before an 18-month-long bear market, which deflated the index to 14,309, a 63% decline. The Nikkei has traded above 20,000 only a few times since 1992 and closed the year 2000 at less than 14,000. It may be a long time before the Internet sector recovers.

The More Things Change...

… the more *people* stay the same! Market bubbles are not recent phenomena. Nor are they uncommon.

One of the most impressive market bubbles occurred in Holland in the 1630s.[4] What makes this bubble so amusing is that the commodity that was so highly sought after was the tulip bulb. Over a five-year period, tulip bulb mania inflated bulb prices to the point where one bulb was worth 10 times a yoke of oxen. A tulip bulb costing nearly $100,000? An out-of-town sailor inadvertently popped the tulip bulb price bubble. Mistaking a bulb for an onion, he ate it. Wondering whether the bulbs were worth the high prices, people erupted into a panic and within a week the bulbs were almost worthless.

Modern market bubbles have common elements. Given the statement below, how would you fill in the blank?

> We are in a new era. _____ has ushered in a new type of economy. Those stuck in the old ways will quickly fall away. Traditional company valuation techniques do not capture the value of this revolution.

Given the nature of this chapter, you probably said The Internet. However, if you lived in 1850, The railroad would have been the best answer. If you lived in the 1920s, you might have said The Federal Reserve System ushered in a new economy. In the mid-1950s, the answer would have been The New Deal. Even as recently as 1990, you might have said biotechnology created a new type of economy. In each case, the people became irrationally exuberant over the idea that a new technology or government would make the old economy obsolete. The exuberance fuels a great bull market which precedes a great decline.

Price bubbles are not uncommon, nor is each one unique. The specific details may change, but the basic principles are always the same.

There are certain factors that contribute to the mania that causes market bubbles:

- **Short-term focus.** During a market bubble, your mind-set is more like that of a trader than an investor. Instead of buying a stock because you think the company's products, market share, and management will be dominant in the future, you buy a stock because you think the price will rise in the next week, day, or hour. The firm's products, market share, and management become ancillary, or even irrelevant. Take Sharon, for example. She was interviewed by the PBS show *Frontline*.[5] She invested her family's entire life savings into two tiny technology stocks, most of it in one company. "To tell you the truth, I don't even know the name of it. I know the call letters are AMLN; it's supposed to double by August," she says. For the record, AMLN is Amylin Pharmaceuticals. During the several months before the airing of *Frontline*, Amylin traded at around $12 a share. By August it was trading at under $8 a share and it closed the year at $5.43 a share. Needless to say, Sharon wasn't too pleased.

- **Faith.** "Things are different this time." "The old valuation measures are no longer appropriate." These common comments occur during the formation of a market bubble because the high prices cannot be justified with traditional measures. When the scale says you have gained 30 pounds, the problem is obvious—your scale no longer works. During a market bubble, you invest on the basis of faith, not due diligence.

- **Social validation.** You want to talk about it. Investing talk has become popular at social occasions. I have already discussed the online discussion groups. But also consider the expansion of talk radio investment shows and the call-in questions to CNBC. During a market bubble, investing becomes social.

Stock market bubbles do not occur because of new economics or new technologies; they occur because of people's psychology. New economics and new technology are only the rallying cry for the bubble. When your overconfidence (in Chapters 2 and 3) combines with your emotions (Part 2), you have a problem. When everyone is caught up in his or her own psychology, the problem is magnified.

Stock market bubbles happen because of human psychology.

THE BOILER ROOM GOES ONLINE

In the old days, unscrupulous brokers tried to separate people from their money by setting up operations in the basement (boiler room) of some building and calling prospective victims. Sales pitches were developed to convince people to buy the stock of some obscure company, overpriced gold coins, or oceanfront property in Arizona. It was relatively easy to defend against these boiler rooms: just like you tell your children—don't talk to strangers.

However, there is a new and different breed of scam artist. These scam artists are not different in the scams they perpetrate, only in the way they execute these scams. The Internet and the recent mania surrounding dotcoms have allowed scams to flourish. No longer are boiler rooms needed. No need for phone lines and time-wasting phone conversations. All these scammers need is a computer and a few minutes.

The age-old stock scam is the *pump and dump*. In the past, an unscrupulous broker would buy shares of a tiny company, which would start to push up the stock price. Then the broker calls you to recommend the stock, saying you had better buy it quickly because it is already climbing (the pump). As more and more investors buy, the price gets pushed way up. The broker sells his shares (the dump) into this high demand at the inflated price and makes a killing. He stops pumping the stocks because he is out. The price plummets back to the original level and you take the big loss.

When you lose your rational thought and get too affected by your psychological biases, you become a target.

Today, the same scheme is perpetrated with several online bulletin board postings. Instead of making hundreds of phone calls to reach investors, investors willingly go to the postings. The next time you read a message touting a stock, remember that it could be from someone like Jonathan Lebed, the 15-year-old high school boy from New Jersey. He would buy shares in a tiny stock and then pump it in the after-hours chat rooms. While he was in school, the excitement would build on the Web bulletin boards, attracting investors to buy the stock, starting the upward price spiral. Jonathan would then dump his shares at the inflated price, and all the investors who took the bait on his scam would be left holding the loser when the stock price returned to normal levels. He made hundreds of thousands of dollars from these scams. It doesn't feel very good to get scammed by a teenager. However, the anonymity of the online chat rooms means you do not know who you are dealing with. The SEC gets 300 emails a day complaining about such scams.[6]

While many investors are wise enough not to take the postings on chat sites seriously, there are other ways you can lose your money. The Internet has fostered a new type of stock scam known as the *info bomb*. Many investors get their news from traditional news wire services (Reuters, Dow Jones, Business Wire, etc.) that distribute news stories and company announcements. An info bomb is a planted false story that is inadvertently circulated by reputable news services or made to appear that it originated at one of these services. The story is planted to cause a big move in the stock price of a company.

Take, for example, the fake Bloomberg News page announcing a takeover bid of PairGain Technologies. An employee at PairGain created and distributed the phony story. Investors flocked to PairGain hoping to cash in on a quick profit, causing the stock price to soar 30%. Many investors got burned when PairGain officials denied the takeover bid and the stock quickly dropped.

Or consider the info bomb planted by Mark Jakob, a 23-year-old community college student. Mark had been short Emulex stock for several months. (A short position profits when stock prices fall and loses money when stock prices rise.) Emulex stock had risen. So, after quitting a job at online wire service Internet Wire, Mark planted a story on the system to the effect that the Emulex CEO was resigning amid an accounting scandal. The other news wires picked up the story, and the company's stock price quickly plunged 62%. By the time Emulex was able to deny the hoax, Mark had closed his short position at a huge profit. Then he bought shares at the low price and made another huge profit when the stock climbed back to prehoax levels. His total profits were $250,000. As is common with this type of fraud, the FBI caught him before he could spend any of the money. However, that isn't much comfort to investors who panicked and sold Emulex stock when it dropped into the $40 range, only to see it climb back to over $100 a share after the hoax was revealed.

So, how do you steer clear of market mania and investment scams? You are vulnerable to both of these investing pitfalls because of your psychological biases. The first step toward avoiding destructive behavior is to understand its cause, which means you should understand your psychological biases. Hopefully, what you've read so far has helped you to do just that. The next part of this book will tell you about your willpower and introduces rules of thumb for controlling biases and avoiding problems.

ENDNOTES

1. Andrew Edgecliffe, 1999, "eToys Surges after Listing," *Financial Times*, May 21: 29.

2. Michael Cooper, Orlin Dimitrov, and Raghavendra Rau, 2000, "A Rose.com by Any Other Name," *Journal of Finance*, to be published.

3. T. Ewing, "Mistaken Identity Bolsters Shares of Tiny Company," 1999, *Wall Street Journal*, April 1: C1.

4. Robert Sobel, 1965, *The Big Board: A History of the New York Stock Market*, New York: The Free Press.

5. "Betting on the Market," *Frontline*, January 4, 1997.

6. Daniel Kadlec, 2000, "Crimes and Misdeminors," *Time*, October 2: 52–54.

5

What Can I Do about It?

14 Self-Control, or the Lack of It!

Milestones

- Short-Term versus Long-Term Focus
- Controlling Ourselves
- Self-Control and Saving
- Self-Control and Investing
- Self-Control and Dividends
- Summing Up

A common adage on Wall Street is that the markets are motivated by two emotions: fear and greed. Indeed, this book suggests that investors are affected by these emotions. However, acting out of fear or greed is rarely the wise move. The decision that will benefit you over the long term is usually made in the absence of strong emotions. You will face a lifelong struggle choosing between decisions that make the present more enjoyable and those that will make the future more enjoyable. Many decisions require balancing

> **Three years of losses often turn investors with thirty-year horizons into investors with three-year horizons; they want out.**
>
> **Kenneth Fisher and Meir Statman[1]**

this trade-off. Do you read this chapter now or later? Do you purchase a new stereo or invest the money for the future?

The self-control problem can be thought of as the inter-action or conflict between your two selves—the *planner* and the *doer*. The doer (your emotional side) wishes to consume now instead of later and to procrastinate on unpleasant tasks, acting on desire. The planner (your rational side) wishes to save for later consumption, show will power, and complete unpleasant tasks now.[2]

Fortunately people recognize the fact that they some-times lack willpower and that this can lead to spur-of-the-moment decisions. Our soci-ety is full of examples of people recognizing they need help with self-control, such as

> **The conflict between desire and willpower occurs because you are influenced both by long-term rational concerns and by more short-term-ori-ented emotional factors.**

diet clinics, Alcoholics Anonymous, drug abuse treatment programs. In fact, we are often willing to *pay* for help.

SHORT-TERM VERSUS LONG-TERM FOCUS

In general, you like to receive rewards early and put off unpleasant tasks until later. However, this attitude depends on the circumstances. Consider this example.[3] If people are asked on February 1 whether they would prefer to do seven hours of an unpleasant task on April 1 or eight hours of the unpleasant task on April 15, people prefer to do the lesser work on April 1. However, if given the same choice on the morning of April 1, most people decide to delay the work until April 15 even though it means doing more total work. When making decisions involving the present, you often procrastinate, even when it causes you to do *more* work later.

This attitude can also affect your investment decision making.

People seem to view the present very differently than they view the future. This leads to strong desire and weak willpower.

For example, most people would rather get $50 immediately than $100 in two years, forgoing a 41% annual return. Alternatively, almost no one prefers $50 in four years to $100 in six years even though this is the same choice, albeit four years into the future.[4]

CONTROLLING OURSELVES

Most people want to maintain self-control and implement decisions that provide benefits over the long term. However, oftentimes desire is stronger than willpower, prompting people to employ many techniques to help them have willpower. I categorize these techniques into two groups: *rules of thumb* and *environment control.*[5] These techniques can help you to reduce desire and increase willpower.

Rules of Thumb

Rules of thumb can help you to control your behavior. You can create these rules during times when your willpower is high and emotions are at a low ebb. During situations with high emotion and desire, you can rely on these rules to remind you how to exert willpower. Consider these common rules.

- To control spending: *don't borrow money.*
- Also to keep spending down: *fight the urge to splurge.*
- Recovering alcoholics use: *not one drop.*

- Retired people who don't want to outlive their money control spending with: *don't touch the principal.*
- Employees should contribute to their 401(k) plan and refrain from spending the money early through loan programs. To remember the importance of this strategy: *save much, don't touch.*
- To control emotional biases and trading behavior, investors: *buy low, sell high.*
- To maintain a long-term perspective during bear markets: *stay the course.*

Environment Control

You can also control your environment to help with willpower. Common ways to control the environment are to remove desired objects from the area or avoid situations that are likely to cause self-control problems. Common examples are:

- People on a diet will not keep cookies in the house.
- Gambling addicts will avoid going to Las Vegas.
- People that are always late set their watch a few minutes ahead.
- People who have trouble getting out of bed place the alarm clock across the room to force themselves to get up.
- Forgetful or unorganized people make lists to help them get things done.

People are often willing to incur costs in order to maintain self-control. For example, professional athletes earn the vast majority of their income during a short time period. After earning millions of dollars, some end up bankrupt because they could not control their desires. To help with willpower, some athletes hire agents to impose limits on their consumption. For another example consider the average smoker. Most smokers recognize that they should not smoke too much (or at all). In order to avoid smoking too much, most smokers buy cigarettes by the pack because the easiest way to control the number of cigarettes smoked is to control the number available. But this technique causes higher spending on cigarettes since it's more expensive to buy by the pack than by the carton. Nevertheless, smokers are willing to pay the extra cost in order to control their environment in the pursuit of stronger willpower.

SELF-CONTROL AND SAVING

Saving for retirement is difficult because it requires self-control. Before the rise of the 401(k) plan in the late 1970s and the socialization of investing (see Chapter 7), 51% of retired people had no income from financial assets. Only 22% of retirees earned investment income that contributed more than 20% of their total retirement income. Most of the retirees had succumbed to the desire of current consumption during their peak earning years and procrastinated saving for the future.[6]

If you're like most people, you probably find it easier to save from a lump-sum payment than from regular income. Consider two people who each earn $25,000 per year. The first is paid the $25,000 in 12 equal monthly payments. The second person earns $20,000 divided into 12 monthly payments and then receives a $5,000 bonus paid all at once. Since both people earn the same for the year, they should both save the same amount for retirement. However, the person with the bonus will probably save more. It is easier to come up with the disposable income to save with a lump-sum payment (or cash windfall). Saving money from a monthly salary requires much more self-control. This may be why the savings rate of countries like Japan is higher than in the United States. A higher percentage of income in Japan is paid in year-end bonuses. It is easier to live on regular income and to save windfalls.

People recognize that a $50 increase in their monthly income is likely to be spent. The equivalent, a $600 tax refund, has a greater chance of being saved.

This may also explain the U.S. taxpayer's propensity for giving interest-free loans to the government. Most people have too much withheld for taxes throughout the year and then receive a tax refund in the spring. In 1996, approximately 76% of individual taxpayers overpaid an aggregate $117 billion on their taxes. That is a lot of forgone interest!

You can easily adjust your withholding rate and retain more of your income during the year. However, you may actually *prefer* to overpay. In an experiment using MBA students and a case of a hypothetical wage earner, 43% of the 132 students chose to pay more than the minimum required quarterly tax payment.[7]

IRAs

The individual retirement account (IRA) and the corporate 401(k) pension plan are two savings innovations that can help you save and invest for the future. These plans are simple to implement and give you the added benefit of an immediate tax reduction. Additionally, the large penalties for early withdrawal help you with the willpower to keep the money invested for retirement. Most people who invest in an IRA or a 401(k) plan contribute again the following year; i.e., they form a habit to help their willpower.

It is clearly rational to contribute to an IRA. The investment earnings in an IRA grow tax deferred—you do not pay income or capital gains taxes on the profits in the year in which they are earned. Instead, you pay income taxes when you take the money out of the IRA after you retire. Therefore, it is best to contribute the money to the IRA as soon as possible to let it grow. For a particular tax year, you should contribute on January 1 of that year to get the maximum time benefit of the money growing. However, you probably do not have the self-control to invest early in the year. The tax laws allow contributions made as late as April 15 of the next year to count as the previous year's IRA. Indeed, most taxpayers contributing to an IRA will not contribute until the last few months before the IRA deadline. They need the deadline to exert self-control.

401(k) Plans

Contributing to your 401(k) plan is also a very smart thing to do. Usually employers contribute at least some percentage of what the employee is contributing—e.g., if your company has 50% matching, for every $1.00 you put into your 401(k), the company puts in 50¢. Right off the top, before any money is invested, you've had a *guaranteed* return of 50%. If a broker told you she had a stock for you that would give you a guaranteed 50% return the same day you bought it, you'd be running for the checkbook! Also consider that the 401(k) contribution is in pretax dollars. When you contribute $1, you get to keep the full $1 and get a 50¢ match. However, if you get the $1 in your paycheck instead, you get only 65¢ after federal, state, and social security taxes are taken out. Which do you prefer, $1.50 in investments or 65¢ in your pocket? Most people's excuse for not signing up is that they can't afford it, but they really can't afford *not* to. However, since the inception of the 401(k), the most difficult aspect for plan administrators is getting employees to sign up and begin contributing in the first place. This is because people procrastinate even in the face of something that would give them huge returns! The more important the decision, the more likely it is that people will procrastinate.

Another reason for procrastination regarding 401(k)s may be related to the different investment options—employees often feel they can make a better decision about which options to choose if they just take a little more time to analyze the choices. This continuous delay costs the employee the two most important factors in building a retirement nest egg: time and invested capital. This problem is getting worse because companies are increasing the number of options available in 401(k) plans. These plans started out having three or four choices (typically, company stock, money market fund, bond fund, and stock fund). However, many plans now have mutual fund families with hundreds of different funds from which to select. Having more options available induces more procrastination. In order to help employees with self-control, some companies, as mentioned earlier in this book, are now automatically signing employees up for 401(k) contributions when they are first hired. That way, while employees procrastinate on how to change the automatic contribution defaults, they are still contributing and investing.

SELF-CONTROL AND INVESTING

Psychological factors affect not only your ability to save, but also your investing. Problems from overconfidence, aversion to regret, and pride seeking cause you to make poor decisions. If you recognize this problem, you can use rules of thumb and/or environment control like we discussed earlier to help with investing self-control. For example, if you like to trade actively, you may realize this behavior is not optimal in the long term. As a compromise between the two selves (the planner and the doer), you open two brokerage accounts. One is for the majority of your wealth to implement a long-term buy-and-hold strategy, while you can use the other to "have fun." Of course, you could actively trade a small portion of your overall wealth all in just one account, but it would require self-control to actively trade only a small amount of capital. Having two accounts helps with self-control.

Many investors have neglected to practice self-control. Instead of controlling their environment, they have done just the opposite—they're letting the Internet environment control them. Online traders are using information obtained in chat rooms to make investment decisions, decisions that are usually irrational because they are spur-of-the-moment decisions based on rumor, not on information (see Chapters 12 and 13).

> **Unscrupulous brokers invoke fear, greed, pity, and other emotions to cause you to abandon your usual deliberation process in favor of a quick decision to buy whatever the broker is selling.**

Unfortunately, the dark side of the financial services industry understands that behavioral aspects often drive investors' decisions. Boiler room brokers use high-pressure sales tactics designed to manipulate emotions and influence your behavior. You should have rules of thumb to help you avoid falling into their trap. Rules like

- Never buy investments from a broker you don't know.
- Never buy investments when the broker calls you. Investments that brokers are selling hard are rarely the type of investments you should be buying.

SELF-CONTROL AND DIVIDENDS

Here is a long-standing puzzle in traditional finance: Why do individuals have a strong preference for cash dividends? This is especially puzzling considering that dividend income is taxed at a higher marginal rate than capital gains.

Consider the example demonstrated in Table 14.1. You own 1,000 shares of a $100 stock (a total value of $100,000). If the stock pays a 1% dividend, then you receive $1,000 and the stock price falls to $99 per share (the 1,000 shares are now worth $99,000). The decrease in the stock price is the amount of the dividend paid. However, if you are in the 28% tax bracket, then you keep only $720 after taxes. In sum, you end up with $720 in cash and stock worth $99,000.

Now consider the alternative. Assume that the stock does not pay a dividend. If you want some cash, you must sell 10 shares at $100 a share to receive the $1,000 proceeds, thus creating your own dividend. This is called a *homemade dividend*. You are now left with 990 shares of a stock worth $100, for a total of $99,000. If the stock sold has no capital gains liability, then you owe no taxes and keep the

REAL DIVIDENDS VERSUS HOMEMADE DIVIDENDS

	Received Dividend	Homemade Dividend
Table 14.1		
Starting number of shares owned	1,000	1,000
Beginning price per share	$100	$100
Beginning stock value	$100,000	$100,000
Per share dividend	$1	$0
Pretax dividend income	$1,000	
Dividend by selling 10 shares		
Selling shares pretax income		$1,000
Ending number of shares	1,000	990
Price per share	$99	$100
Ending stock value	$99,000	$99,000
Taxes		
Income Tax (28% marginal rate)	$280	$0
Capital Gains Tax (20% rate, 50% gain)	$0	$100
After Tax Income	$720	$900

entire $1,000 in cash. Note that you are better off creating your own dividend. If the stock had a cost basis of $50 a share and capital gains are taxed at 20%, then $100 is owed in taxes. You are still better off making your own dividends.

If you wish to maximize your wealth and cash flow, you should seek income through homemade dividends rather than cash dividends. However, people seem to prefer cash dividends. This behavior seems irrational in traditional finance, but it can be explained by investor psychology. Consider the following case:

> Because of the steep rise in oil prices in 1973, Consolidated Edison Company of New York experienced a large decline in income. Consequently, that year they omitted paying the dividend, which had been paid for 89 consecutive years. At the 1974 annual meeting, angry shareholders confronted management, demanding a restoration of the dividend. Widows queried, "Who is going to pay my rent?" People claimed that they were going to have to survive on only their Social Security checks.[8]

Why didn't these people simply create homemade dividends? There are two psychological traits that explain this behavior: mental accounting and self-control. First, making homemade dividends probably didn't even occur to these investors. Mental accounting (Chapter 8) causes investors to separate investments into different mental accounts. When investing for income, investors buy high-dividend stocks, bonds, and annuities (Chapter 9). A different mental account and investment strategy is used for capital gains. It is difficult to think of a stock in the income mental account as having the potential to capture a capital gain.

These mental accounts can be useful for investors who need to exert self-control. A retired person may recognize that her wealth needs to outlive her—i.e., she doesn't want to outlive her money. Because she may be tempted to spend too much money, she enacts a common rule of thumb to help with self-control: *never touch the principal*. This rule is a helpful reminder to avoid overspending. However, it can also inhibit creative thinking that increases income—like homemade dividends. Therefore, sometimes it pays to bend the rules a bit.

SUMMING UP

You may need to invoke self-control management techniques, such as making rules of thumb and controlling your investment environment. These techniques can help you avoid the mistakes caused by letting your emotions and psychological biases influence your investment decisions. However, you should also understand why the rules exist and be able to bend them if creative thinking allows you to increase your wealth. Chapter 15 reviews your psychological biases and proposes some specific strategies, rules of thumb, and management techniques that help you to overcome those biases to improve your wealth.

ENDNOTES

1. P. 92 of Kenneth Fisher and Meir Statman, 1999, "A Behavioral Framework for Time Diversification," *Financial Analysts Journal,* May/June: 88–97.

2. This discussion is from Richard Thaler and Hersh Shefrin, 1981, "An Economic Theory of Self-Control," *Journal of Political Economy* 89: 392–406.

3. This example is proposed in Ted O'Donoghue and Matthew Rabin, 1999, "Doing It Now or Later," *American Economic Review* 89(1): 103–24.

4. George Ainsle, 1991, "Derivation of 'Rational' Economic Behavior from Hyperbolic Discount Curves," *American Economic Review* 81(2): 334–40.

5. These ideas are explored in Richard Thaler and Hersh Shefrin, 1981, "An Economic Theory of Self-Control," Journal of Political Economy 89: 392–406; Stephen Hoch and George Loewenstein, 1991, "Time-Inconsistent Preferences and Consumer Self-Control," *Journal of Consumer Research* 17: 492–507.

6. George Akerlof, 1991, "Procrastination and Obedience," *American Economic Review* 81(2): 1–19.

7. Benjamin Ayers, Steven Kachelmeister, and John Robinson, 1999, "Why Do People Give Interest-Free Loans to the Government? An Experimental Study of Interim Tax Payments," *Journal of the American Taxation Association* 21(2): 55–74.

8. This case is summarized from Hersh Shefrin and Meir Statman, 1984, "Explaining Investor Preferences for Cash Dividends," *Journal of Financial Economics* 13: 253–82.

15

Battling Your Biases

Milestones

- Strategy 1: Understand Your Psychological Biases
- Strategy 2: Know Why You Are Investing
- Strategy 3: Have Quantitative Investment Criteria
- Strategy 4: Diversify
- Strategy 5: Control Your Investing Environment
- Additional Rules of Thumb
- In Conclusion

Remember the day-trader cartoon in Chapter 1? The roller coaster called "The Day Trader" represents the modern investment environment. The roller coaster has dramatic highs and lows. As a modern-day investor, you can experience strong emotional highs and lows. This emotional roller coaster has a tendency to enhance your natural psychological biases. Ultimately, this can lead to bad investment decisions.

The previous chapter began the discussion of how to overcome your psychological biases. It introduced two strategies of exerting self-control: *rules of thumb* and *environment control*. This chapter proposes strategies for controlling your environment and gives you specific rules of thumb that focus you on investing for long-term wealth and on avoiding short-term pitfalls caused by decisions based on emotions.

The first strategy was proposed in Chapter 1: Understand the psychological biases. We have discussed many biases in this book. You may not remember each bias and how it affects you (due to cognitive dissonance and other memory biases—see Chapter 10), so reviewing them here should be beneficial. In fact, to help you make wise investments long after reading this book, you should re-familiarize yourself with these biases next month, next year, and every year.

STRATEGY 1: UNDERSTAND YOUR PSYCHOLOGICAL BIASES

In this book, there are three categories of psychological biases: *not thinking clearly, letting emotions rule,* and *functioning of the brain.* Let's review the biases in each category.

Not Thinking Clearly

Your past experiences can lead to specific behaviors that harm your wealth. For example, you are prone to attribute past investment success to your skill at investing. This leads to the psychological bias of *overconfidence*. Overconfidence causes you to trade too much and to take too much risk. As a consequence, you pay too much in commissions, pay too much in taxes, and are susceptible to big losses.

The *attachment bias* causes you to become emotionally attached to a security. You are emotionally attached to your parents, siblings, children, and close friends. This attachment causes you to focus on their good traits and deeds. You also tend to discount or ignore their bad traits and deeds. When you become emotionally attached to a stock, you also fail to recognize bad news about the company.

When taking an action is in your best interest, the *endowment bias* and *status quo bias* cause you to do nothing. When securities are

THE EFFECTS OF YOUR PSYCHOLOGICAL BIASES.

Table 15.1

Psychological Bias	Effect on Investment Behavior	Consequence
Overconfidence	Trade too much	Pay too much in commissions and taxes
Overconfidence	Take too much risk and fail to diversify	Susceptible to big losses
Attachment	Become emotionally attached to a security and see it through rose-colored glasses	Susceptible to big losses
Endowment	Want to keep the securities received	Not achieving a match between your investment goals and your investments
Status Quo	Hold back on changing your portfolio or starting your 401(k)	Failure to adjust asset allocation and begin contributing to retirement plan
Seeking Pride	Sell winners too soon	Lower return and higher taxes
Avoiding Regret	Hold losers too long	Lower return and higher taxes
House Money	Take too much risk after winning	Susceptible to big losses
Snake Bit	Take too little risk after losing	Lose chance for higher return in the long term

given to you, you tend to keep them instead of changing them to an investment that meets your needs. You also procrastinate on making important decisions, like contributing to your 401(k) plan.

In the future, you should review these psychological biases. Keep this book and Table 15.1 handy for this purpose.

Letting Emotions Rule

Emotions get in the way of making good investment decisions. For example, your desire to feel good about yourself—*seeking pride*—causes you to sell your winners too soon. Trying to *avoid regret* causes you to hold your losers too long. The consequences are that you sell the stocks that perform well and keep the stocks that

THE EFFECTS OF YOUR PSYCHOLOGICAL BIASES (CONTINUED).

Psychological Bias	Effect on Investment Behavior	Consequence	Table 15.1
Get Even	Take too much risk trying to break even	Susceptible to big losses	
Social Validation	Feel that it must be good if others are investing in the security	Participate in a price bubble which ultimately causes you to buy high and sell low	
Mental Accounting	Fail to diversify	Not receiving the highest return possible for the level of risk taken	
Cognitive Dissonance	Ignore information that conflicts with prior beliefs and decisions	Reduces your ability to evaluate and monitor your investment choices	
Representativeness	Think things that seem similar must be alike. So a good company must be a good investment.	Purchase overpriced stocks	
Familiarity	Think companies that you know seem better and safer	Failure to diversify and put too much faith in the company in which you work	

perform poorly. This hurts your return and causes you to pay higher taxes.

When you are on a winning streak, you may feel like you are playing with the *house's money*. The feeling of betting with someone else's money causes you to take too much risk. On the other hand, losing causes emotional pain. The feeling of being *snake bit* causes you to want to avoid this emotional pain in the future. To do this, you avoid taking risks entirely by not owning any stocks. However, a diversified portfolio of stocks should be a part of everyone's total investment portfolio. Experiencing a loss also causes you to want to *get even*. Unfortunately, this desire to get even clouds your judgment and induces you to take risks you would not ordinarily take.

And finally, your need for social validation causes you to bring your investing interests into your social life. You like to talk about investing. You like to listen to others talk about investing. Over time, you begin to misinterpret other people's opinions as investment fact. On an individual level, this leads to investment decisions based on rumor and emotions. On a societal level, this leads to price bubbles in our stock market.

Functioning of the Brain

The manner in which the human brain functions can cause you to think in ways that induce problems. For example, people use *mental accounting* to compartmentalize individual investments and categorize costs and benefits. While mental accounting can help you exert self-control to not spend money you are saving, it also keeps you from properly diversifying. The consequence is that you assume more risk than necessary to achieve your desired return.

To avoid regret about previous decisions that did not turn out well, the brain filters the information you receive. This process, called *cognitive dissonance*, adjusts your memory about the information and changes how you recall your previous decision. Obviously, this will reduce your ability to properly evaluate and monitor your investment choices.

The brain uses shortcuts to reduce the complexity of analyzing information. These shortcuts allow the brain to generate an estimate of the answer before fully digesting all the available information. For example, the brain makes the assumption that things that share similar qualities are quite alike. *Representativeness* is judgment based on stereotypes. Furthermore, people prefer things that have

**Figure
15.1**

"You are so stubborn."

some *familiarity* to them. However, these shortcuts also make it hard for you to correctly analyze new information, possibly leading to inaccurate conclusions. Consequently, you put too much faith in stocks of companies that are familiar to you or represent qualities you desire.

This review of the psychological biases should help you with the first strategy of understanding *your* psychological biases. However, as Figure 15.1 suggests, knowing about the biases is not enough. You must also have a strategy for overcoming them.

STRATEGY 2: KNOW WHY YOU ARE INVESTING

You should be aware of the reasons you are investing. Most investors largely overlook this simple step of the investing process, having only some vague notion of their investment goals: "I want a lot of money so that I can travel abroad when I retire." "I want to make the money to send my kids to college." Sometimes people think of vague goals in a negative form: "I don't want to be poor when I retire." These vague notions do little to give you investment direction. Nor do they help you avoid the psychological biases that inhibit good decision making.

It is time to get specific. Instead of a vague notion of wanting to travel after retirement, be specific. Try

> A minimum of $75,000 of income per year in retirement would allow me to make two international trips a year. Since I will receive $20,000 a year in Social Security and retirement benefits, I will need $55,000 in investment income. Investment earnings from $800,000 would generate the desired income. I want to retire in 10 years.

Having specific goals gives you many advantages. For example, by keeping your eye on the reason for the investing, you will

- Focus on the long term and look at the "big picture"
- Be able to monitor and measure your progress
- Be able to determine if your behavior matches your goals

For example, consider the employees of Miller Brewing Company who were hoping to retire early (discussed in Chapter 11). They had all their 401(k) money invested in the company stock, and the price of the stock fell nearly 60%. When you lose 60%, it takes a 150% return to recover the losses. It could easily take the Miller employees many years to recover the retirement assets. What are the consequences for these employees? Early retirement will probably not be an option.

Investing in only one company is very risky. You can earn great returns or suffer great losses. If the Miller employees had simply compared the specific consequences of their strategy to their specific investment goals, they would have identified the problem. In this type of situation, which option do you think is better?

A. Invest the assets in a diversified portfolio of stocks and bonds that will allow a comfortable retirement in two years.

B. Invest the assets in the company stock, which will either earn a high return and allow a slightly more comfortable retirement in two years, or suffer losses which will delay retirement for seven years.

Whereas option A meets the goals, option B gambles five years of work for a chance to exceed the goal and is not much different than placing the money on the flip of a coin.

STRATEGY 3: HAVE QUANTITATIVE INVESTMENT CRITERIA

Having a set of quantitative investment criteria allows you to avoid investing on emotion, rumor, stories, and other psychological biases. It is not the intent of this book to recommend a specific investment strategy like *value* investing or *growth* investing. There are hundreds of books that describe how to follow a specific style of investing. Most of these books have quantitative criteria.

Here are some easy-to-follow investment criteria:

- Positive earnings
- Maximum P/E ratio of 50
- Minimum sales growth of 15%
- A minimum of five years of being traded publicly

If you are a value investor, then a P/E maximum of 20 may be more appropriate. A growth investor may set the P/E maximum at 80 and increase the sales growth minimum to 25%. You can also use criteria like profit margin and PEG ratio, or you can even look at whether the company is a market share leader in sales.

Just as it is important to have specific investing goals, it is important to write down specific investment criteria. Before buying a stock, compare the characteristics of the company to your criteria. If it doesn't meet your criteria, don't invest!

Consider the Klondike Investment Club of Buffalo, Wyoming, discussed in Chapter 7. The club's number one ranking stems in part from its making buy decisions only after an acceptable research report has been completed. Klondike's criteria have protected its members from falling prey to their psychological biases. On the other hand, the California Investors Club's lack of success is due partially to the lack of criteria. Its decision process leads to buy decisions that are ultimately controlled by emotion.

I am not suggesting that qualitative information is unimportant. Information on the quality of a company's management or the types of new products under development can be useful. If a stock meets your quantitative criteria, then you should next examine these qualitative factors.

STRATEGY 4: DIVERSIFY

The old adage in real estate is that there are three important criteria when buying property: location, location, location. The investment adage should be very similar: diversify, diversify, diversify.

It is not likely that you will diversify in a manner suggested by modern portfolio theory and discussed in Chapter 9. However, if you keep some simple diversification rules in mind, you can do well.

- **Diversify by owning many different types of stocks.** You can be reasonably well diversified with 15 stocks that are from different industries and of different sizes. One diversified mutual fund would do it too. However, a portfoilio of 50 technology stocks is not a diversified portfolio, nor is one of five technology mutual funds.

- **Own very little of the company you work for.** You already have your human capital invested in your employer—that is, your income is dependent on the company. So diversify your *whole self* by avoiding that company in your investments.

- **Invest in bonds, too.** A diversified portfolio should also have some bonds or bond mutual funds in it.

Diversifying in this way helps you to avoid tragic losses that can truly affect your life. Additionally, diversification is a shield against the psychological biases of attachment and familiarity.

STRATEGY 5: CONTROL YOUR INVESTING ENVIRONMENT

If you are a recovering alcoholic, you should not go out to bars with your drinking buddies. If you are on a diet, you should not leave a dish of M&M's on the table. If you want to overcome your psychological investment biases, you must control your investment environment.

Do you check your stocks every day? Every hour? So many people are doing this that companies are limiting their employees' Internet access so that they are not distracted by looking up their investments all day. To control your environment, you need to limit those activities that magnify your psychological biases. Here are some tips you can use to help to control your environment.

- **Check your stocks once a month.** By checking your stocks once a month instead of once an hour, you inhibit your behavioral reactions of feeling snake bit, seeking pride, and playing with the house's money.

- **Make trades only once a month and on the same day of the month.** Pick one day of the month, like the 15th, and place buy and sell trades only on that day of the month. This helps you avoid the misconception that speed is important. Speed is only important if you want to chase a stock on a rumor and get into it just before its bubble bursts. On the other hand, trading once a month helps to overcome overconfidence trading and info bombs.

- **Review your portfolio annually and compare it with your specific goals.** When you review your portfolio, and you should do this on an annual basis, keep in mind the psychological biases of status quo, endowment, representativeness, and familiarity. Does each security in your portfolio contribute both to meeting your investment goals and to diversification? In addition, keep records so that you can overcome cognitive dissonance and other memory biases.

If you just can't bear to do these things, then you are probably addicted to the gambling aspects of playing the market. You should consider taking a small amount of your portfolio and placing it in its own brokerage account. This will be your play money. It should be money that you do not need to pursue your investment goals.

If you do set aside some play money, definitely put it in its own account. This is an important aspect to controlling your environment. If you don't keep it separate this way and instead decide to play with a small amount of money in your main brokerage account, you will no doubt be tempted to use more. If you have some successes in your playing, remember that it is probably just luck. Playing the market (as opposed to investing) is like playing a slot machine in Las Vegas. You win, or you lose, but skill has nothing to do with it. And, on average, you lose. Of course this makes sense now, but it is hard to believe when you are winning.

ADDITIONAL RULES OF THUMB

Also consider implementing these rules to shield you from your own psychological biases.

- **Avoid stocks selling for less than $5 a share.** Most investment scams (particularly the pump and dump scheme) are conducted in these penny stocks.

- **Chat rooms and message boards are for entertainment purposes only!** It is on these boards that your overconfidence is fostered, familiarity is magnified, and artificial social consensus is formed.

- **Before you place a trade on a stock that does not meet your criteria, remember that it is unlikely that you know more than the market.** Investing outside of your criteria implies that you have some informational advantage over others. Are you sure you know more?

- **Have a goal to earn the market return.** Most active trading is motivated by the desire to earn a higher return than everyone else is earning. The strategies for earning a higher return usually foster psychological biases and ultimately contribute to lower returns. However, the strategies for earning the market return, like fully diversifying, are successful because they inhibit your biases.

- **Review Table 15.1 annually.** This action will re-enforce Strategy 1: Understand your psychological biases.

IN CONCLUSION

Successful investing is more than simply knowing all about stocks. Indeed, understanding yourself is equally important. Investors who think they are knowledgeable frequently fail because they allow their psychological biases to control their decisions. In the first chapter of this book, I proposed overcoming this problem by reading this book, which was written to help you

- Learn the many psychological biases that affect decision making
- Understand how these biases affect investment decisions
- See how these bias-affected decisions can reduce your wealth
- Learn to recognize and avoid these biases in your own life

I hope this book has given you the knowledge, motivation, and strategies to overcome your own psychological biases and become a successful investor.

401(k) plan, 37–40, 42, 67, 119–120, 129, 149, 151–152, 161, 164. *See also* individual retirement account

A

Amazon.com, 62, 68, 125
American Association of Individual Investors, 105
America Online, 24, 125
American Stock Exchange, 115
Ameritrade, 126, 129
Amylin Pharmaceuticals, 139
Appian Technology, 136–137
AppNet Systems Inc., 136–137
arbitrage, 7, 8
asset allocation, 38–40, 119
asset class, 96
attachment bias, 35, 40–41, 160
AT&T, 70, 117

B

Barber, Brad, 25, 26, 29
Barron's, 106
Barton, Mark, 131–132
Beardstown Ladies, 71–72
bear market, 29
behavioral portfolios, 96–98
Bell Atlantic Corp, 70
beta, 29, 93
bias
  attachment, 35, 40–41, 160
  endowment effect, 3, 35–37, 160
  home, 117–118
  status quo, 3, 35, 37–40, 160

biotechnology, 59
Block Trading Inc., 132
Bloomberg News, 141
boiler room, 140, 153. *See also* scams
bonds, 92–93, 94, 95, 96. *See also* corporate bonds; high-yield bonds; Treasury bills; Treasury bonds
breaking even, 59, 108
Brewer, Barry, 28
Broadway Trading LLC, 131
brokerage, discount, 25, 50
brokers, online, 126, 129–130
Bronsteen, William, 28
bubbles, 42, 62–63, 137–140
bulletin board, 23, 68, 127, 136, 141, 168. *See also* chatroom
bull market, 14, 29, 61
business owners, 13–14

C

California Investors club, 74, 165
capital gains, 48, 153–155
Castle Convertible Fund, 70
chatroom, 68, 127. *See also* bulletin board
Cisco, 129
CNBC, 19, 68, 70, 139
Coca-Cola, 118
cognitive dissonance, 103–106, 161, 162. *See also* memory
coin toss, 18, 57–58, 59
Color Tile Inc., 119
commissions, 27
commodities, 92, 94

Compaq Computer, 116

Computer Literacy Inc. *See*
    fatbrain.com

Consolidated Edison Company, 154

corporate bonds, 92, 94

correlation, 89, 90

Czech Value Fund, 70

D

Dartboard column (*Wall Street
    Journal*), 14

Datek Online, 129

day trading, 9, 126, 130–132, 159

debit cards, 82

debt aversion, 82

discount brokerage, 25, 50

disposition effect, 47–49, 51–52, 72,
    84, 161

diversification, 42, 89–96, 117–118,
    119, 132, 166

dividends, 7, 153–155
    homemade, 153–155

doer (vs. planner), 147

Dole, Elizabeth, 35

dotcoms, 42, 135–137

Dow Jones Industrial Average, 7, 71,
    138

E

earnings warning, 17–18

eBay, 62, 135

emerging market stocks, 92, 94

Emulex, 141–142

endowment effect, 3, 35–37, 160

environment control, 148, 149, 159,
    166–167. *See also* self-control

eToys, 62, 135

E*TRADE, 126, 129

Europe and East Asian stocks, 92, 94,
    96

exuberance, 135, 136–137

F

faith, 139

familiarity, 113, 116–120, 161
    401(k) plans, 119–120
    international, 117–118
    investing, 117–120

fatbrain.com, 136

fear, 147, 153

Federal Reserve, 8

Financial Times, 70

futures traders, 53–54

forecasts, 5

G

gambling, 60, 58, 59, 117, 132, 167

gender, investment styles by, 25, 71

General Motors Corp, 132

Germany, and status quo bias, 37, 120

glamor stocks, 114–115

Government Finance Offers
    Association, 96

Graham, Benjamin, 23

greed, 147, 153

Greenspan, Alan, 135

growth investing, 165

H

hedge fund, 7–8

herding, 68–69

high-yield bonds, 92, 94. *See also*
    bonds

Holland, and market bubble, 138

home bias, 117–118

homemade dividend, 153–155

house money effect, 57–58, 160, 162

Hulbert Financial Digest, 67–68

I

illusion, 4–5

illusion of control, 18–19, 23–25,
    30–31, 126, 128, 130
    active involvement, 19, 24

choice, 18, 24
information, 19, 24, 130
outcome sequence, 18, 24
task familiarity, 18–19, 24
illusion of knowledge, 14–18, 30–31,
        126, 128, 130
individual retirement account
        (IRA), 28, 151. *See also*
        401(k)
info bomb, 19, 141. *See also* scam
inheritance, 36
initial public offerings (IPOs), 50,
        60–61, 136–137
Intel, 129
International Business Machines
        (IBM), 48
Internet, 9, 23, 30–31, 125–133,
        135–142
    day trading, 31, 130–132
    information, 126–127
    magnifying biases, 126
    message boards, 23, 127
    overconfidence, 30–31, 126,
        127,128–129
    performance, 130
    scams, 140–142
investment clubs, 37, 71–74, 92, 165
    Beardstown Ladies, 71–72
    dynamics, 73–74
    Klondike, 73, 165
    performance, 72
investment environment ("roller
        coaster"), 9
investment socialization, 68, 106–107,
        108, 139
Iomega, 23–25
IRA. *See* individual retirement
        account

J

Jakob, Mark, 141–142
Japan, 117–118, 138, 150

K

Kahneman, Daniel, 57
Klondike Investment Club, 73, 165
Korn, Gary, 132

L

Lebed, Jonathan, 141
loans, 84
Long Term Capital Management, 7–8
losers, 50–51, 85
lottery, 47

M

mania, 138
Mannix, Norma, 58–59
markets
    bear, 29
    bull, 14, 29, 61
Markowitz, Harry, 89, 98
Massmutual Corporate Investors, 70
MCI Communications, 70
media, 106, 129–130
memory, 101–103, 110
    cognitive dissonance, 103–106, 161,
        162
    investments, 102–103, 104–105
    socialization, 106–107
mental accounting, 79–86, 89–98, 155,
        162
    budgeting, 80–82
    diversification, 89–98
    investing, 84–85
    portfolios, 89–91
    risk, 91–95, 96, 98
mental budgeting, 80–82
Meriwether, John, 7
Merton, Robert, 7
message boards. *See* bulletin boards
Microsoft, 17, 48, 125
Miller Brewing Company, 119, 164
modern portfolio theory, 8, 89, 95
momentum, 116, 127

Morningstar, 125
Motley Fool, 23, 125, 127
Mullins, David, 7
mutual funds, 30, 40, 104, 105–106,
    116, 152, 166

N

Nasdaq, 61, 137–138
National Association of Investors Corp
    (NAIC), 71, 72
newsletters, 67–68
New York Stock Exchange, 31, 52, 70,
    115
Nikkei Index, 138
Nobel prize, 7, 89
Northwest Airlines, 85

O

Odean, Terrance, 25, 26, 29, 50
opinions, 24, 68
online brokers, 126, 129–130
overconfidence, 12–20, 22–32, 72, 160
    driving, 13
    experience, 29
    Internet, 30–31, 126, 127, 128–129
    learning, 14
    luck and, 131–132
    risk, 28–29
    starting a business, 13–14
    trading, 25, 26–28, 128–129, 130
overreaction, 114
owners, business, 13–14

P

Pacific Gas and Electric, 119
pain, 47, 52, 83, 101–102, 107
PaineWebber Group, 29
PairGain Technologies, 141
Park, Charles, 24
P/E ratio, 115, 135, 165
Philip Morris, 119–120

planner (vs. doer), 147
portfolios, 25, 89–91, 93, 95, 96–98,
    117, 166, 167
portfolio theory. *See* modern portfolio
    theory
prediction, 5–7
Price Waterhouse, 71
pride, 47, 51. *See also* disposition effect
procrastination, 3
Procter & Gamble, 40–41
public pension systems, 96
pump and dump, 140–141, 168. *See
    also* scams
pyramid of assets, 96–97

R

racetrack, psychology at, 59, 103
Raging Bull, 127
real estate, 92, 94, 96
reference points, 107–108
regret, 47–49, 52–54, 69, 108
    of commission, 47
    of omission, 47
representativeness, 113–116, 162
    investing, 114–116
    momentum, 116
    stereotypes, 113
return, 7–8, 9, 27, 42, 49–50, 71, 89,
    95, 98, 104–105, 116, 130,
    136, 168
risk, 7–8, 28–29, 30, 60, 89, 90, 91–95,
    96, 116. *See also*
    overconfidence
rules of thumb, 148–149, 152, 155,
    159, 168. *See also* self-control
Russell 2000 Growth Index, 92, 93–94
Russia, 8

S

Salomon Brothers, 7
S&P 500 Index, 31, 72, 104, 119

scams, 140–142, 153, 168
  info bombs, 19, 141–142
  pump and dump, 140,–141.
  See also boiler room
Scholes, Myron, 7
Schwab Online, 126
Securities and Exchange Commission
    (SEC), 60, 106, 136, 141
self-control, 3, 146–156, 159–169
  401(k) plans, 151–152
  environment, 148, 149, 159,
    166–167
  investing, 152–153
  rules of thumb, 148–149, 152, 155,
    159, 168
  saving, 150.
  See also environment control
selling winner, 48, 49–51
short-term focus, 139, 148
Silicon Investor, 125, 127
small-cap stocks, 92, 94
smoking, and environment control,
    149
snake bit, 49, 58–59, 162
socialization, 68, 73–74, 106–107, 108,
    130. *See also* investment
    socialization; memory
standard deviation of return, 92–94.
    See also risk
status quo bias, 3, 35, 37–40, 160
Steadman funds, 105–106
stereotypes, 113. *See also*
    representativeness
stocks
  emerging markets, 92, 94
  Europe and East Asian, 92, 94,
    106
  glamor, 114–115
  small cap, 92, 94
  value, 114–115, 127, 165
stop-loss order, 53
sunk costs, 82–83

T

taxes, 48, 150, 151–152, 153–154
  loss selling, 53, 129
  tax swap, 85
Teach Me to Trade, LLC, 129–130
Tele-Communications Inc., 70
The Street.com, 138
Toys "R" Us, 135
Treasury bills, 8, 36, 92–94. *See also*
    bonds
Treasury bonds, 8, 95. *See also* bonds
tulip bulb, and market bubble, 138
turnover, 25–28, 30, 31, 106, 128–129
Tversky, Amos, 57

U

United Airlines, 85
United Kingdom, 117–118
U.S. savings bonds, 30–31

V

valuation, 62–63
Value Line, 73, 125
value investing, 165
value stocks, 114–115, 127, 165
VerticalNet, Inc., 60–61

W

willpower, 147, 148
windfall, 58, 150
winners, 48, 49–51

Y

Yahoo!, 125, 127, 135

Z

Zip drive, 23–24

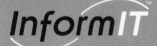

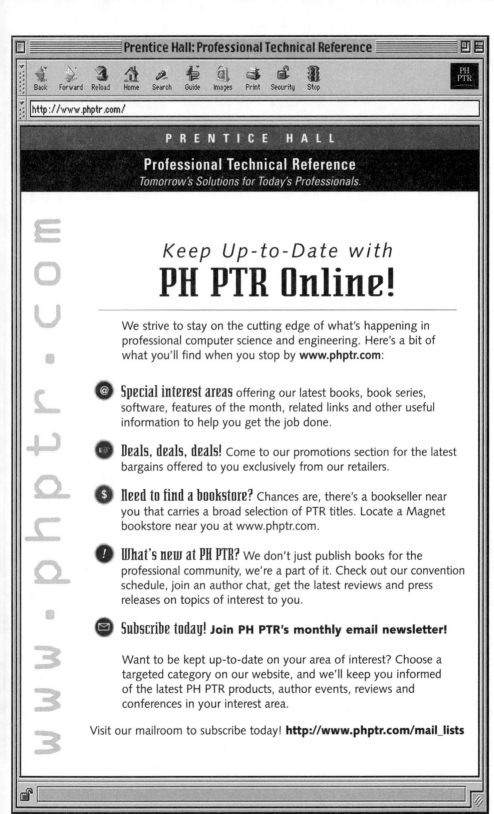